Workbook

WORLD ENGLISH 2

Real People • Real Places • Real Language

Kristin L. Johannsen

W0114870

HEINLE
CENGAGE Learning™

Australia • Brazil • Japan • Korea • Mexico • Singapore • Spain • United Kingdom • United States

HEINLE
CENGAGE Learning™

World English 2 Workbook
Real People • Real Places • Real Language
Kristin L. Johannsen

Publisher: Jason Mann

Commissioning Editor: Carol Goodwright

Development Editor: Louisa Essenhigh

Technology Development Manager: Debie Mirtle

Director of Global Marketing: Ian Martin

Product Manager: Ruth McAleavey

Content Project Editor: Amy Smith

ELT Production Controller: Denise Power

Cover Designer: Page 2 LLC

Compositor: MPS Limited, A Macmillan Company

Head of Production and Manufacturing: Alissa Chappell

ISBN: 978-1-111-21772-3

Heinle, Cengage Learning
Cheriton House
North Way
Andover
Hampshire
SP10 5BE
United Kingdom

Cengage Learning is a leading provider of customized learning solutions with office locations around the globe, including Singapore, the United Kingdom, Australia, Mexico, Brazil, and Japan. Locate your local office at: **international.cengage.com/region**

Cengage Learning products are represented in Canada by Nelson Education, Ltd.

Visit Heinle online at **elt.heinle.com**

Visit our corporate website at **www.cengage.com**

Cover photo: Kenneth Garrett/National Geographic Image Collection, Karnak, Egypt

Printed in China
3 4 5 6 7 8 9 10 – 15 14 13 12 11

CONTENTS

	Grammar	Vocabulary	Communication	Reading and Writing
Food from the Earth page 7				
UNIT 1	Verb tense review: Simple present tense vs. present continuous tense Simple past tense (regular and irregular)	Geographical regions Climate Food staples	Describing land, climate and food Identifying linking sounds	"Sweet History" Describing a favorite food
Communication page 13				
UNIT 2	Present perfect tense Signal words: *yet*, *already*, *ever*, *never*	Culture, communication, and gestures Small talk	Making small talk: first day of class	"Drinking Tea, Breaking the Ice" Meeting a new person
Cities page 19				
UNIT 3	Future with *will* *Will* + time clauses	City life Maps	Describing neighborhoods	"Forests for Cities" Describing a beautiful urban site
The Body page 25				
UNIT 4	Review of comparatives, superlatives, and equatives Infinitive of purpose	Human organs Parts of the body Everyday ailments	Describing one's health Identifying linking sounds	"In the *Death Zone* of Mount Everest" Writing about a favorite sport and its effects on the players
Challenges page 31				
UNIT 5	Simple past tense vs. past continuous tense *Enough*, *not enough*, *too* + adjective	Physical and mental challenges Phrasal verbs	Describing an achievement Identifying –*ed* sounds	"How do you spell . . . " Writing about an admired person
Transitions page 37				
UNIT 6	Simple past tense vs. present perfect tense *How* + adjective or adverb	Stages of life Adjectives for age: *youthful*, *childish*, *mature*	Discussing a friend's life transition Identifying ə sounds	"Celebrating Transitions" Writing a paragraph to describe a life transition

	Grammar	Vocabulary	Communication	Reading and Writing
Luxuries page 43				
UNIT 7	Present passive voice Passive voice with *by* (present tense)	Luxury ítems Import/export items Past participles of irregular verbs	Expressiong opinions and giving reasons	"Where does silk come from?" Choosing a luxury prize
Nature page 49				
UNIT 8	Real conditionals in the future Quantifiers (review)	Nouns and adjectives to describe animals Adverbs of manner	Offering alternatives to solve a specific problem Identifying sentence phrases	"Elephants or People?" Expressing an opinion about harmful animals
Life in the Past page 55				
UNIT 9	*Used to/would* Past passive voice	Activities and artifacts Indian innovations Separable phrasal verbs	Describing life in the past and comparing it with present day life	"Living History at Jamestown Settlement" Writing about an important historical place
Travel page 61				
UNIT 10	Modals of necessity Modals of prohibition	Travel preparations Vacations At the airport	Choosing a vacation destination	"Letters to the Editor" Writing an opinion on the desirability of increased tourism
Careers page 67				
UNIT 11	Modals for giving advice Indefinite pronouns	Career decisions Participial adjectives	Giving career advice Creating a job profile	"Dream jobs: Mona Davis" Writing about a *dream job*
Celebrations page 73				
UNIT 12	*As … as* *Would rather*	Festivals and holidays Greetings for celebrations	Describing holidays Identifying intonation patterns	"The Oldest Celebration in the World" Writing about a special celebration or tradition

Illustration

7, 8: (all) Keith Neely/IllustrationOnLine.com; **11:** National Geographic Maps; **13:** (all) Ralph Voltz/IllustrationOnline.com; **15:** Keith Neely/IllustrationOnLine.com; **16:** National Geographic Maps; **25:** Sharon&Joel Harris/IllustrationOnLine.com; **27:** (b, all) Mark Collins/IllustrationOnline.com; **31:** (all) Ralph Voltz/IllustrationOnline.com; **33:** Mark Collins/IllustrationOnline.com; **43, 47:** (all) Jim Atherton; **49:** (tl) Jim Atherton, (tr) Joseph/Shutterstock, (b, both) Ted Hammond/ IllustrationOnline.com; **50, 51:** (all) Ted Hammond/IllustrationOnLine.com; **56:** Keith Neely/IllustrationOnLine.com; **61, 62, 64:** Nesbitt Graphics, Inc.; **67, 68:** Ralph Voltz/IllustrationOnline.com; **73:** Keith Neely/IllustrationOnLine.com; **77:** National Geographic Maps

Photo

9: photos.com; **10:** (t) Howard Sandler/Shutterstock, (m) Carol Gering/ iStockphoto, (b) Ronald Sumners/Shutterstock; **12:** Susan Seubert/ National Geographic Image Collection; **14:** Monkey Business Images/ Shutterstock; **16:** (both) Image courtesy Greg Mortenson, Central Asia Institute; **18:** Brad Killer/iStockphoto;

19: Imaani1000/Dreamstime; **20:** (l to r) Arpad Benedek/iStockphoto, Carole Gomez/iStockphoto, RTimages/Shutterstock, Terry W Ryder/ Shutterstock, Péter Gudella/Shutterstock;

21: Jami Garrison/iStockphoto; **22:** (t) Japan National Tourism Organization, (b) Courtesy of The Forestry Commission; **24:** Imaani1000/ Dreamstime; **26:** photostogo; **27:** (t, l to r) Alex Bramwell/Dreamstime, Nikola Hristovski/Dreamstime, Suzanne Tucker/Shutterstock, Gene Chutka/iStockphoto; **28:** (both) Barry Bishop/National Geographic Image Collection; **30:** iStockphoto; **32:** Charles Shapiro/Dreamstime;

34: (both) Alex Wong/Getty Images; **36:** Kevin Krug/National Geographic Image Collection; **37:** (t) David Grossman/Alamy (b, l to r) Martin Novak/ Shutterstock, Ilja Mašík/Dreamstime, Suprijono Suharjoto/Dreamstime, Vincent Yu/AP Images, Monkey Business Images/Shutterstock; **38:** Monkey Business Images/ Shutterstock; **39:** Monkey Business Images/Shutterstock; **40:** (t) Gerd Ludwig/National Geographic Image Collection, (m) Norbert Michalke/age fotostock, (b) Tibor Bognar/Alamy; **42:** Zurijeta/Dreamstime; **44:** (t to b) Monkey Business Images/ Shutterstock, photostogo, Stephen Coburn/Shutterstock, Sasha Radosavljevich/Shutterstock; **45:** (l to r) Paul Cowan/Dreamstime, Sir Armstrong/Shutterstock, Derek Latta/iStockphoto, photos.com; **46:** (t) Radu Razvan/Shutterstock, (m) Robert Churchill/iStockphoto, (b, both) iStockphoto; **48:** Mark Evans/iStockphoto; **49:** (tl) David Huntley/Shutterstock, (tr) iStockphoto, (ml) Steffen Foerster Photography/ Shutterstock, (mr) EcoPrint/ Shutterstock, (bl) Rich Carey/Shutterstock., (br) Eric Isselée/iStockphoto; **52:** (t) Michael Nichols/National Geographic Image Collection, (m) Friedrich Stark/Alamy, (b) Tim Fitzharris/Minden Pictures/National Geographic Image Collection; **53:** Michael Nichols/ National Geographic Image Collection; **54:** Paul Morton/iStockphoto; **55:** North Wind/North Wind Picture Archives; **57:** (l to r) photos.com (4), H. Tom Hall/National Geographic Image Collection; **58:** (tl) Richard Gunion/iStockphoto, (tm) The Art Archive/British Museum/Harper Collins Publishers, (tr) Ira Block/National Geographic Image Collection, (b) The Art Archive/ Musée de la Marine Paris/Gianni Dagli Orti; **60:** North Wind/ North Wind Picture Archives; **61:** Lee Torrens/Shutterstock; **62:** (l to r) Robert Houser/JupiterImages, Chrislofoto/Shutterstock, John Kernick/ National Geographic Image Collection; **63:** ABC Photo/Shutterstock; **64:** (t) photos.com, (m) Monkey Business Images/Dreamstime, (b) Varina and Jay Patel/ Shutterstock; **65:** photos.com; **66:** ABC Photo/ Shutterstock; **69:** matka_Wariatka/ Shutterstock; **70:** Image99/ JupiterImages; **71:** (t & m) photostogo, (b) Ben Blankenburg/ iStockphoto; **72:** Hongqi Zhang/Dreamstime; **73:** Ilya D Gridnev/Shutterstock; **74:** (l to r) Rahalariva786/Dreamstime, Paul Cowan/Dreamstime, Kaphoto/ Dreamstime, Laura Nadina Samson/Dreamstime, Nasser Bu-hamad/Dreamstime; **75:** (tl) Juriah Mosin/Shutterstock, (tr) Creativeapril/Shutterstock, (ml) Pavel Losevsky/ iStockphoto, (mr) SuperStock/JupiterImages, (b) Andres Rodriguez/Dreamstime; **76:** (t) Dainis Derics/iStockphoto, (b) Ulf Slunga/iStockphoto; **78:** Andrew Rich/iStockphoto.

Lesson A

A. Complete the sentences with words from the box.

meal	staple food	geography	climate	flat	humid
farmer	region	coastal	grasslands	mountainous	crop

1. Most people in China eat rice every day. It's their _____.

2. Abbas is a _____ in Oman. He grows fruits and vegetables.

3. Lunch is the biggest _____ of the day in Mexico. People eat it at about two o'clock.

4. In my country, summer is very rainy and _____. The air feels wet all the time.

5. The land in Holland is very _____. There aren't any mountains there.

6. Many parts of Australia have a hot, sunny _____. The usual weather there is very nice.

7. Switzerland is a _____ country. Many tourists go there to see the Alps and to go climbing.

8. Argentina produces very good beef because cattle live on the _____ there.

9. Coffee is a famous _____ in Brazil.

10. The north of Canada is very cold. Not many people live in that _____.

11. The _____ of a country is its land and climate.

12. In the _____ part of my country, people eat a lot of fish, because they are near the ocean.

B. Look at the pictures. Use the phrases to write sentences in the simple present and present continuous tenses.

▲ usually

1. have dinner/at home/in a restaurant

   a. __Usually, Claudia has dinner at home.__

   b. __Tonight, she is having dinner in a restaurant.__

2. eat fish and rice/pizza and salad

   a. _____

   b. _____

3. drink water/cola

   a. _____

   b. _____

4. wear a t-shirt/a nice jacket

   a. _____

   b. _____

5. watch TV/talk to her friends

   a. _____

   b. _____

▲ tonight

Lesson B

A. Read about food in China. Complete the text with words from the box.

staple food	climate	regions	land	mountainous

China is a very large country with several important _____. In the northeast, the _____ is very cold. The _____ is flat. People there eat a lot of wheat bread. The south of China is hot and humid. Some parts are _____. Rice is the _____ there.

B. Write sentences about the land, climate, and food in two parts of India.

▲ **North India: wheat bread**

1. (land) _____

2. (climate)_____

3. (food)_____

▲ **South India: rice**

1. (land) _____

2. (climate)_____

3. (food)_____

C. When a word ends in a consonant sound and the next word starts with a vowel sound, the words are linked together. Read each sentence out loud. Mark two places where the words are linked together.

1. He has a brother in Tokyo.
2. I always eat a sandwich for lunch.
3. We never take a vacation in winter.
4. Rice is the staple food in Korea.
5. My English teacher is from Australia.
6. Most of the students live in the city.
7. We work in that office together.
8. Do you have any brothers or sisters?

Lesson C

A. Unscramble the names of these staple foods. Circle the foods you sometimes eat.

1. ecri _____
2. tosa _____
3. bcalk sneba _____
4. ncro _____
5. thewa _____
6. tilmel _____
7. nosysabe _____
8. llisnte _____
9. soopatet _____
10. smay _____
11. caucy _____
12. dre naebs _____

B. Complete the chart with the simple past tense form of each verb. Use your dictionary if necessary.

Present tense	Past tense	Present tense	Past tense
1. go		9. send	
2. say		10. write	
3. buy		11. find	
4. know		12. get	
5. fly		13. eat	
6. take		14. drink	
7. see		15. fall	
8. tell		16. give	

C. Answer the questions. Write complete sentences in the simple past tense.

1. What did you eat for dinner last night?

   _____

2. What did you do during your summer vacation last year?

   _____

3. What did you do last week? (three things)

   _____

4. Where did you go last weekend?

   _____

D. Complete the email. Use your own information.

Hi!

You asked me about a traditional dish in my family. I really like _____. It's made from

_____ and _____. We eat it on special days like _____.

In my family, _____ usually cooks this dish. I hope you can try it sometime!

Your friend, _____

Sweet History

Chocolate is a new food, but a very old drink. About 3000 years ago, the Maya people in Honduras began growing cacao trees. They used the seeds to make a bitter, spicy drink. They mixed the seeds, called "cocoa beans," with chile peppers and water and put spices in the drink. They drank chocolate on special days. It was also a medicine for stomach problems. In Mexico, the people liked chocolate so much that they used cocoa beans for money.

In the early 1500s, Spanish explorers went to Mexico. They brought chocolate back to Europe on their ships. It became a very popular drink for rich people in Spain. The Spanish didn't mix the cocoa beans with chiles. They put in other ingredients like sugar and vanilla to make it sweet. Later, the English added milk to the drink. In London, there were "chocolate houses." People could sit there and enjoy a cup of hot chocolate with their friends.

The first chocolate candy was made in the 1700s. Inventors in Switzerland made a machine to produce hard chocolate. But people made the candy by hand, so it was very expensive. Candy didn't become cheap until there were machines to make it. Factories in England made the first modern chocolate bars in 1847. In 1868, a company called Cadbury started selling boxes of chocolate candies.

Today, chocolate is popular in nearly every country in the world. Every year, we eat almost 6 million tons of it! It is one of the world's favorite foods.

A. How did chocolate move around the world? Write numbers 1–5 on the places on the map.

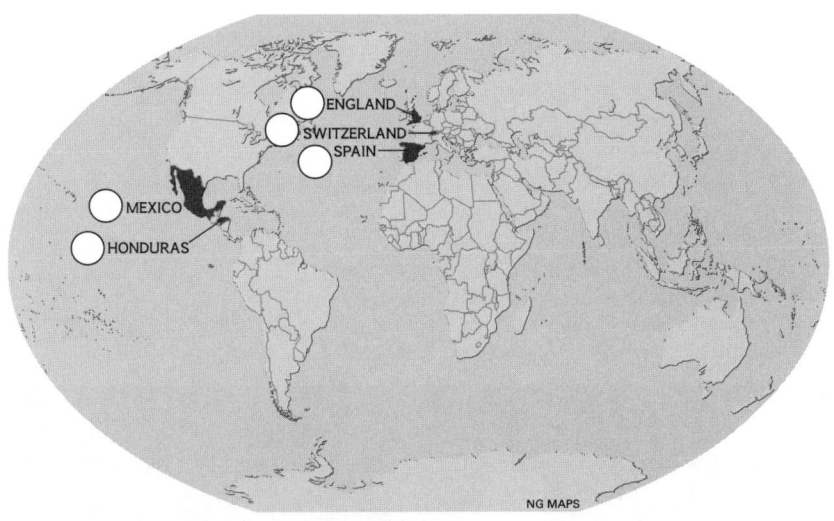

B. Read the article again. Circle **T** for *true* or **F** for *false*.

1.	The first chocolate was a drink.	T	F
2.	The Maya people's chocolate had the same taste as chocolate today.	T	F
3.	People in Switzerland made the first sweet chocolate.	T	F
4.	People went to chocolate houses in England to drink chocolate.	T	F
5.	The first chocolate candy was very cheap.	T	F
6.	Machines made the first chocolate bars in 1868.	T	F

C. Answer the questions.

1. How often do you eat chocolate? _____

2. Is chocolate popular in your country? _____

3. Do you think chocolate is good for your body? Why, or why not? _____

_____

D. Write about one of your favorite foods. Where do people make it or grow it? When do you eat it? Why do you like it?

_____

_____

_____

_____

_____

Review

Complete the crossword puzzle using vocabulary and grammar from this unit.

Across

4. people use this food to make bread
7. the usual weather in a place
10. a plant that people grow on farms
11. simple past tense of *write*
12. simple past tense of *go*
13. a part of a country
15. near the ocean
17. simple past tense of *tell*
18. simple past tense of *buy*

Down

1. simple past tense of *know*
2. simple past tense of *get*
3. breakfast, lunch, or dinner
5. something that people eat every day (2 words)
6. the staple food in China
7. the staple food in Mexico
8. simple past tense of *see*
9. simple past tense of *find*
14. with no mountains
16. simple past tense of *say*
17. simple past tense of *take*

Lesson A

A. Circle the word that completes the sentence.

1. When I make **small talk** with my neighbor, we talk about (money/the weather).
2. People usually talk to their (boss/friends) in a **formal** way.
3. A **culture** is a group of people with (different/the same) ways of living.
4. A **traditional** food is very (old/new).
5. An **informal** greeting in English is ("Good afternoon."/"Hi.")
6. A **custom** is a way to do things that is (usual/unusual) in a country.
7. When two people **connect**, they (understand/don't understand) each other.
8. A **rule** tells you the (right/wrong) way to do something.

B. Complete the chart with the present perfect form of each verb.

Present tense	Present perfect tense	Present tense	Present perfect tense
1. see	*I have seen*	9. bring	
2. take	*I*	10. come	
3. read		11. make	
4. go		12. eat	
5. be		13. give	
6. cook		14. hear	
7. write		15. do	
8. send		16. buy	

C. Look at the pictures and write questions and answers in the present perfect tense.

1. (be, to Japan) __Have you ever been to Japan?__
   (yes, Kyoto) __Yes, I've been to Kyoto.__

2. (eat Japanese food) _____
   (yes, sushi) _____

3. (go shopping in a Japanese department store) _____
   (yes, Sakura Department Store) _____

4. (visit a Japanese city) _____
   (yes, Kyoto) _____

Lesson B

A. Number the sentences to write a conversation.

_1_ Hi, my name is Abdul Nahas.

___ Really? Which class?

___ It's nice to meet you. I'm Hasna Al.

___ No, not this term. I'm studying art.

___ I'm taking the drawing class. The teacher's name is Ms. Walker. I haven't met her, though.

___ Drawing sounds interesting.

___ Well, this term I'm taking Advanced English Conversation.

___ Nice to meet you too, Hasna. So . . . are you studying English here?

___ What about you? What are you studying?

___ Wow, that sounds interesting too!

B. Write a new conversation. It's the first day of the school term. You're talking to another student and making small talk. Use information about your school.

You: Hi, my _____

Other student: _____

You: _____

Other student: _____

You: _____

Other student: _____

You: _____

Other student: _____

You: _____

Other student: _____

C. Answer the questions.

1. Do you like to make small talk? Why, or why not? _____

   _____

2. What are some good topics for small talk with

   a. a neighbor? _____

   b. a classmate in your school? _____

Lesson C

A. Look at the picture and complete the conversation with the words from the box. You can use the same word more than once.

yet	never	haven't	we've	already	have

Is that Mom?

Mother: Have you eaten dinner _____?

Son: Yes, we have. We've _____ washed the dishes, and _____ cleaned the kitchen. Can we watch a video now?

Mother: Hmmm . . . _____ you done your homework?

Son: We've _____ done some of it. But we _____ finished it _____.

Mother: Well, finish it now! You told me about your big math test tomorrow.

Son: Don't worry. We've _____ gotten a bad grade on a math test!

B. Put the words in the correct order to write a question.

1. like/how/weather/you/this/do _____

2. you/where/from/Angela/do/know _____

3. you/yourself/enjoying/are _____

4. has/long/been/week/a/it _____

5. hear/did/you the accident/about _____

6. waiting/how/you/long/been/have _____

C. Use one of the questions from exercise **B** to write a conversation.

You: _____

Other student: _____

You: _____

Other student: _____

Drinking Tea, Breaking the Ice

An American named Greg Mortenson has written a very popular book with a very unusual title. It's called *Three Cups of Tea*. In it, Mortenson talks about his experiences building schools for poor children in Pakistan and Afghanistan. Why did he do <u>this</u>? And how did the book get its title?

In 1993, Mortenson wanted to climb a mountain in Pakistan called K2. It's 28,251 feet (8611 meters) high. He stayed on the mountain for 70 days, but he couldn't reach the top. After he turned to go down, he became very sick and weak. Two local men took him to a small village called Korphe. <u>There</u>, the Balti people took care of him for seven weeks until he got stronger. To thank the people of the village for their kindness, he decided to build a school in Korphe.

Mortenson worked hard for years to get the money for his first school. Since then, he has built more than 70 schools, and more than 25,000 boys and girls have studied in them. His work was sometimes very difficult, because he was a foreigner and his customs were different. Some men in the villages were very angry with <u>him</u>, because they didn't want schools for girls.

But Mortenson learned about the local cultures, and he found a good way to break the ice: by drinking tea with people. That's where the title of his book comes from. The Balti people have a saying: "The first time you drink tea with a Balti, you are a stranger. The second time you have tea, you are an honored guest. The third time you share a cup of tea, you become family."

By drinking three cups of tea with the people in the mountainous regions of Pakistan and Afghanistan, he could connect with them and learn about their villages and their problems. His schools have brought a better future for the children of the area.

A. Put the events in the correct order.

_1_ Mortenson tried to climb K2.

___ Mortenson wanted to build one school.

___ Mortenson had to come back down.

___ Mortenson went back and built 70 schools.

___ Mortenson wrote a book about his work.

___ Village people took care of Mortenson.

___ Mortenson tried to get money for his first school.

___ Mortenson got sick.

B. Match and complete the sentences in the first column with the correct reason in the second column.

1. Mortenson wanted to build a school　　___ a. because he wanted to connect with them.

2. Mortenson tried to get money　　___ b. because the people in Korphe helped him.

3. Some people didn't like him　　___ c. because he wanted to build a school.

4. Mortenson's work wasn't easy　　___ d. because he built schools for girls.

5. Mortenson drank tea with people　　___ e. because he was from another country.

C. Look at these sentences from the reading. What do the underlined words refer to?

Paragraph 1: Why did he do <u>this</u>?

this = _____

Paragraph 2: <u>There</u>, the Balti people took care of him for seven weeks until he got stronger.

There = _____

Paragraph 3: Some men in the villages were very angry at <u>him</u>, because they didn't want schools for girls.

him = _____

D. Write about a time when you met a new person. How did you break the ice? What did you talk about?

_____

_____

_____

_____

_____

_____

Review

Solve the crossword puzzle with vocabulary and grammar from this unit.

Across

2. past participle of *go*
3. past participle of *be*
5. I haven't cleaned my room.
9. past participle of *see*
10. past participle of *eat*
13. If you look at someone's eyes, you make _____ (2 words)
14. past participle of *take*

Down

1. a group of people with the same way of living
2. past participle of *give*
3. past participle of *buy*
4. past participle of *do*
6. saying hello
7. not formal
8. put two people or things together
9. conversation about things that aren't important (2 words)
11. I've _____ finished all my homework today.
12. past participle of *write*

Lesson A

A. Complete the sentences with words from the box. Use the correct form.

urban	freeway	factory	nightlife
crowded	population	traffic	noisy
rural	suburb	commute	public transportation

1. My city doesn't have much _____. There aren't many cafés or restaurants here.

2. Husain _____ to work every day by bus. It takes 45 minutes.

3. Many people like to live in _____ areas because there are lots of jobs there.

4. I live near the airport, so it's very _____. We can hear planes all night.

5. Nowa always drives on the _____ because it's much faster than the small streets.

6. The _____ of Mexico City is more than 20 million people.

7. My grandparents live on a farm in a/an _____ area. It's very quiet there.

8. This classroom is too _____! We have 40 students in a small room.

9. Nadir lives in a _____ about 15 miles from downtown Dubai.

10. My city has a big problem with _____, because many people have bought cars for the first time.

11. Paris has very good _____. There are buses, trains, and the subway.

12. Eric works in a _____. It makes computers.

B. Write questions about the future with *will*. Then write your predictions.

1. how/people/commute
   How will *people commute?*
   _____

2. most people/live in the city or in the suburbs
   Will _____
   _____

3. cities/be quiet or noisy
   _____
   _____

4. where/people/go shopping
   _____
   _____

5. young people/live in rural areas
   _____
   _____

Lesson B

A. Unscramble the sentences to make a conversation.

(you/how/do/neighborhood/like/in/living/your)

Tim: _____?

(has great nightlife/well/some problems/it/but/there/are)

Jesse: _____ , _____, _____

_____.

(like/what)

Tim: _____?

(it/transportation/have/doesn't/good)

Jesse: _____.

(problem/like/sounds/a/that/pretty big)

Tim: _____.

(the city/but/is building/now/a subway)

(better/we'll/next year/transportation/have)

Jesse: _____

_____. _____.

B. Label the pictures with these expressions about neighborhoods.

| a lot of noise | beautiful old buildings | heavy traffic | serious crime | green space |

1. _____ 2. _____ 3. _____ 4. _____ 5. _____

C. Write a new conversation like the one in exercise **A**. Use expressions from exercise **B** and your own ideas.

You: _____

Your friend: _____

You: _____

Your friend: _____

You: _____

Your friend: _____

_____

Lesson C

A. Circle the correct word to complete each sentence.

1. On some maps, H is a (key/symbol/north) for a hospital.
2. You go to the (museum/library/playground) to get books.
3. Government offices are in the (city hall/museum/post office).
4. On a map, the (scale/symbol/north) shows how big things are.
5. New York is in the (east/west/south) of the United States.
6. We take our old newspapers to the (playground/recycling center/freeway) every month.
7. Look at the (scale/key/direction) to find the meanings of the symbols on the map.
8. My soccer team practices at the (playground/museum/sports center) every week.

B. Draw a map of your neighborhood. Use four symbols to show where things are, and make a key for their meanings.

My neighborhood	Symbol Meaning
	1. _____
	2. _____
	3. _____
	4. _____

C. Circle *before* or *after* to complete the sentence. Then rewrite the sentence using the other word.

1. I'll finish my homework (before/after) I go to bed.
   After I finish my homework, I'll go to bed.

2. We'll invite our neighbors to the meeting (before/after) we choose the date.

3. The reporter will write an article (before/after) she talks to people in the neighborhood.

4. I will look at the map carefully (before/after) I drive downtown.

5. The students will take a practice test (before/after) they have their big exam.

6. We'll go to city hall (before/after) we write a letter about the problem.

Forests for Cities

▲ Kasugayama Forest

You are standing in a beautiful forest in Japan. The air is clean and smells like plants and flowers. There are 175 different kinds of trees, and 60 kinds of birds live here. But you are not in a rural area. You are downtown in the city of Nara, Japan, in Kasugayama Forest, the oldest urban forest in the world. It was started more than a thousand years ago, and today it's very popular with tourists and artists.

Cities around the world are working to protect their urban forests. Some urban forests are parks, and some are just streets with a lot of trees. But all urban forests have many good effects on the environment. Trees take pollution out of the air. They also stop the noise from heavy traffic. They even make the weather better because they make the air 3–5 degrees cooler, and they stop strong winds.

Urban forests also have many good effects on people. They make the city more beautiful. In a crowded area, they give people a place to relax and spend time in nature. In hot countries, urban forests are cool places for walking and other healthy exercise.

In some countries, people are starting new urban forests. In England, there are now 1.3 million trees in an urban forest called Thames Chase, east of London. It was started in 1990, and it has grown very fast. Walking and bicycle clubs use the forest, and there are programs for children and artists. In 2033, it will have 5 million trees.

▲ Thames Chase Forest

Some older cities don't have space for a big urban forest, but planting trees on the streets makes the city better. Scientists found that commuters feel more relaxed when they can see trees. Trees are even good for business. People spend more time at shopping centers that have trees. In the future, urban forests will become even more important as our cities grow bigger. In the megacities of tomorrow, people will need more green space to live a comfortable life. Planting trees today will make our lives better in the future.

A. Find the good effects of urban forests in the article. Complete the chart.

Good effects on the environment:

1. take _____

2. _____

3. _____ because

     a. _____

     b. _____

Good effects for people:

4. _____

5. _____

6. _____

B. Read the article again. Which urban forest do these sentences describe? A sentence can have two correct answers.

	Kasugayama	Thames Chase
1. It's very old.		
2. People are planting trees there now.		
3. Artists go there.		
4. People use it for exercise.		
5. It has many kinds of birds.		
6. It's in the center of the city.		

C. Write about a beautiful place in your city or town. What can you see there? Who goes there? What do you like to do there?

_____

_____

_____

_____

_____

_____

_____

_____

Review

Complete the crossword puzzle using vocabulary and grammar from this unit.

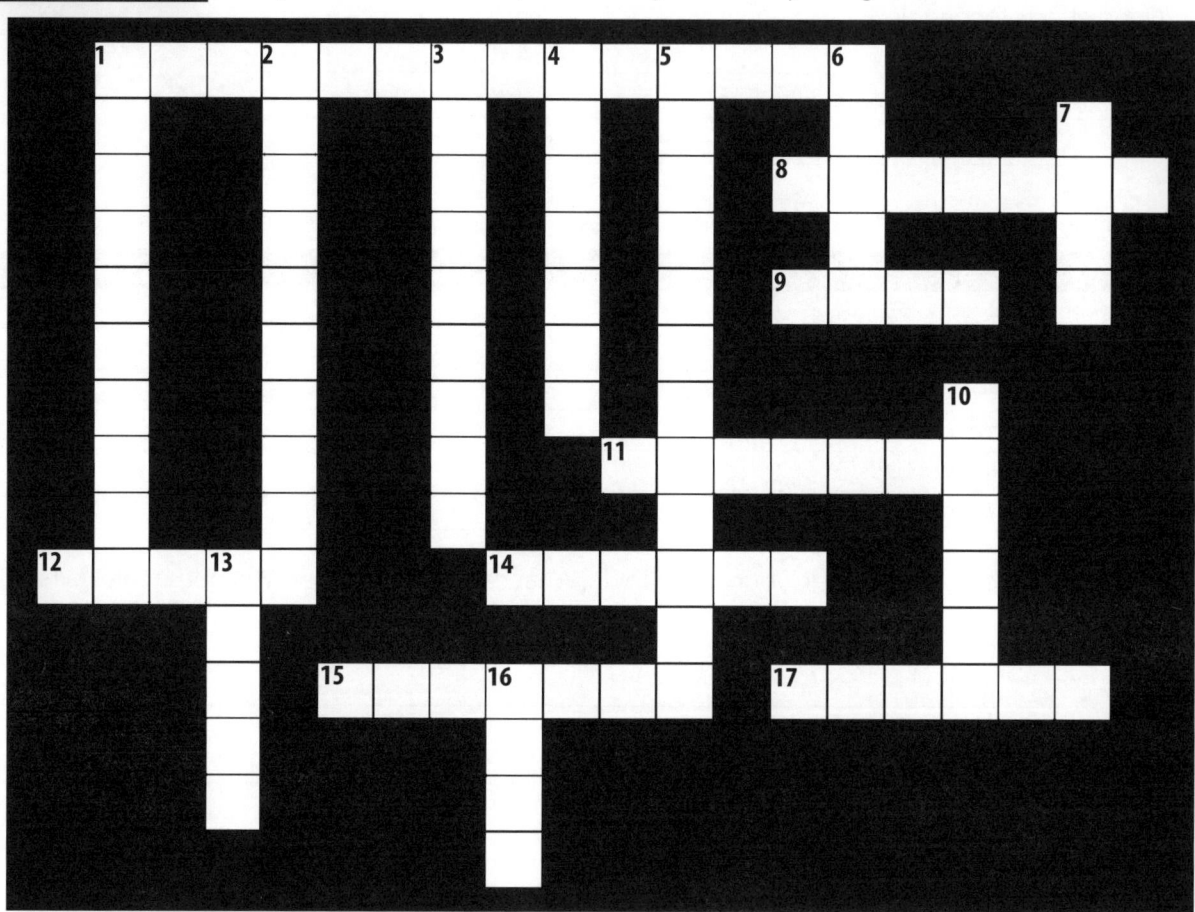

Across

1. a place with many stores (2 words)
8. all the cars in a street
9. a very poor part of a city
11. road where cars go fast
12. an adjective for "in the city"
14. We'll study hard ___ we take the test.
15. with too many people in one place
17. If something is ___, everyone can use it.

Down

1. a very tall building
2. the number of people who live in a place
3. things to do at night
4. travel to work to another place
5. one small part of a city
6. an adjective for "in the country"
7. In the year 2030, more people ___ live in cities.
10. a picture with a special meaning
13. I'll wash the dishes ___ we eat dinner.
16. California is in the ___ of the United States.

Lesson A

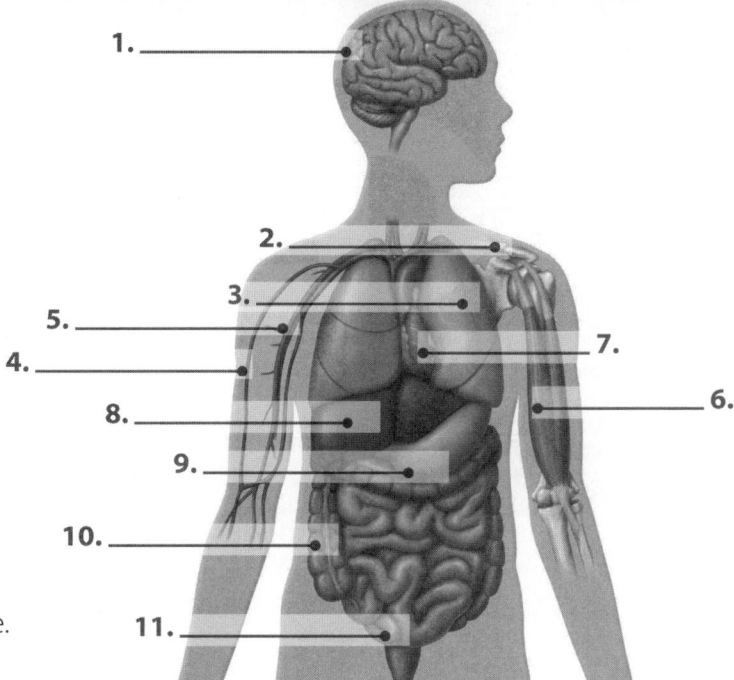

A. Label the parts of the body with the words from the box.

artery	bone	brain
heart	liver	lungs
muscle	small intestine	stomach
large intestine	vein	

1. _____
2. _____
3. _____
4. _____
5. _____
6. _____
7. _____
8. _____
9. _____
10. _____
11. _____

B. Write sentences with the comparative form of each adjective.
Give your opinions.

1. friendly: emails/phone calls
   Phone calls are friendlier than emails.

2. nice: cats/dogs
   _____

3. bad for you: eating junk food/smoking
   _____

4. exciting: basketball/soccer
   _____

5. healthy: meat/vegetables
   _____

6. (adjective: your own idea)
   _____

C. Write your opinion with the superlative form of each adjective.

1. big/problem in the world
   I think pollution is the biggest problem in the world.

2. great/athlete today
   _____

3. healthy/food to eat every day
   _____

4. beautiful/place in our country
   _____

5. enjoyable/way to exercise
   _____

6. (adjective/your own idea)
   _____

Lesson B

A. Answer the questions.

> **How Is Your Health?**
>
> 1. What kinds of exercise do you do? How often?
>   _____
>   _____
>
> 2. Do you have a lot of stress in your life? What causes it?
>   _____
>   _____
>
> 3. Do you think you eat a healthy diet? How could your diet be healthier?
>   _____
>   _____
>
> 4. Are the other people in your family healthy, particularly your parents and grandparents?
>   _____
>   _____
>
> 5. I think my lifestyle is:
>   __ very healthy   __ OK   __ not so healthy   __ very unhealthy
>
> 6. How could you make your lifestyle healthier?
>   _____
>   _____

B. Underline the sounds that are linked together. Then read the sentences out loud.

If the word after -er or more starts with an /r/ sound, the words are linked together.
If the word after -est or most starts with a /t/ sound, the words are linked together.

1. That's the best tomato I've ever tasted.
2. My hardest test was in mathematics.
3. Swimming is more relaxing than running.
4. We need a bigger rug in the living room.
5. He's the newest teacher in our school.
6. We're looking for a better restaurant.

Lesson C

A. Label the pictures with words from the box.

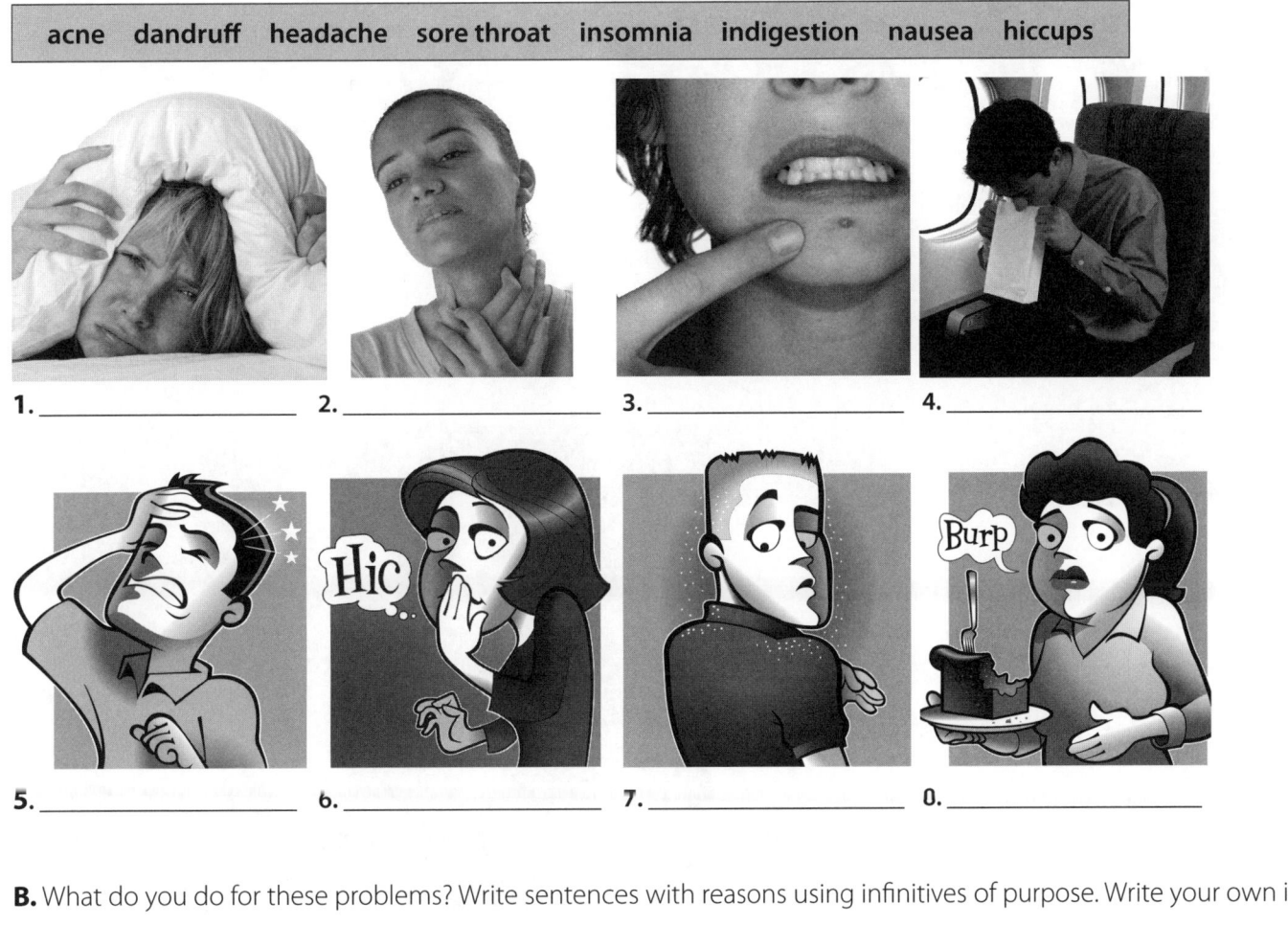

acne   dandruff   headache   sore throat   insomnia   indigestion   nausea   hiccups

1. _____
2. _____
3. _____
4. _____

5. _____
6. _____
7. _____
0. _____

B. What do you do for these problems? Write sentences with reasons using infinitives of purpose. Write your own ideas.

1. indigestion (help)
   I usually *go for a walk* to help indigestion. _____

2. headache (stop)
   _____

3. hiccups (cure)
   _____

4. insomnia (help)
   _____

5. nausea (end)
   _____

6. sore throat (cure)
   _____

7. (your own idea)
   _____

In the *Death Zone* of Mount Everest

Mountain climbers call the part of a mountain over 7000 meters the *Death Zone*. The human body can't live for very long at this height, because the air is too thin and there isn't enough oxygen. Mount Everest, the world's highest mountain, is 8,848 meters high. What happens to the bodies of people who climb it?

Their lungs have to work very hard. Normally, people breathe about 20 times every minute when they are resting. On top of Everest, climbers must breathe 70–80 times a minute to get enough oxygen. The heart must beat faster to move the blood through the veins and arteries. Other parts of the body work very slowly, to save energy. For example, the stomach stops digesting food.

As they get closer to the top of the mountain, climbers feel worse and worse. They have insomnia, so they always feel tired. They get very bad headaches. The sun burns their skin through the thin air, and the bright light from the snow hurts their eyes. Because they have nausea and indigestion, they don't want to eat, and that makes them weaker. In the dry air, they feel thirsty all the time.

Climbing on Everest also affects the brain. Your brain thinks very slowly, because it doesn't have enough oxygen. Scientists have tested this by speaking to climbers with radios. They ask questions like, "If John is taller than Tom, who is shorter?" This is probably very easy for you to answer.

But at the top of Everest, climbers have to think a long time to find the answer, and they often make mistakes. Because the climbers can't think well, they sometimes make bad decisions and get into accidents.

Even with all these difficulties, more than 2500 people have reached the top of Mount Everest. Scientists have found ways to solve some of their problems. Now, almost all climbers breathe from oxygen tanks. They use radios to communicate with people at the bottom, so they can get advice if they're not thinking clearly. There are medicines to help them with headaches and lung problems.

But Mount Everest is still the most difficult and dangerous environment on earth. Almost 200 people have died trying to climb it—with a few more dying every year. Only the strongest bodies can survive up there in the *Death Zone*.

A. Read the article again. Circle **T** for *true* or **F** for *false*.

1. The *Death Zone* is at the bottom of a mountain.   T   F
2. Problems in people's bodies on high mountains come from not having enough oxygen.   T   F
3. Climbing Mount Everest affects many parts of a climber's body.   T   F
4. On Mount Everest, people breathe very slowly because the air is so thin.   T   F
5. Only a few people have climbed Mount Everest.   T   F
6. New inventions have helped solve some health problems on Everest.   T   F
7. Climbers don't die on Mount Everest nowadays.   T   F

B. What happens to these parts of the body in the *Death Zone*? Match the columns.

1. heart ___
2. arteries ___
3. stomach ___
4. brain ___
5. skin ___
6. head ___

a. gets red
b. hurts a lot
c. works very slowly
d. carry blood faster
e. stops working
f. beats very quickly

C. Answer the questions.

1. Why do you think people want to climb Mount Everest?

   _____

   _____

2. What's the highest mountain in your country? Would you like to climb it? Why, or why not?

   _____

   _____

   _____

D. Think about your favorite sport. What happens to people's bodies when they play it? Is it good for their bodies or harmful?

_____

_____

_____

_____

_____

_____

Review

Solve the crossword puzzle with grammar and vocabulary from this unit.

Across

2. the hard parts that support your body
5. the red liquid in your body
9. comparative form of *interesting* (2 words)
11. red spots on your face
12. it covers your body
13. comparative form of *good*
14. the organ that moves your blood
15. your food goes in here
17. you take in air with them

Down

1. not able to sleep
2. the part of your body that thinks
3. Fruit is _____ calories. It doesn't have many calories. (2 words)
4. they make your body move
5. superlative form of *big*
6. it carries the blood from your heart
7. pain in your head
8. the way you live
10. a bad feeling in your stomach
14. Cheese is _____ fat. It has a lot of fat. (2 words)
16. superlative form of *bad*

Lesson A

A. Match the words with their meanings.

1. challenge ____
2. climb ____
3. cross ____
4. extreme ____
5. mental ____
6. physical ____
7. skill ____
8. adventure ____
9. equipment ____
10. goal ____
11. amazing ____
12. achieve ____

a. go up
b. things you need for a particular purpose
c. very surprising and wonderful
d. related to your body
e. related to thinking and your mind
f. something unusual and exciting to do
g. go from one side of something to the other side
h. succeed in making something happen
i. very great in degree
j. something that is new and difficult to do
k. activity that needs special knowledge and practice
l. something you hope to do after some time and effort

B. Write sentences about two events using the simple past tense and past continuous tense.

1. I/take a bath/I/hear the doorbell.

   I was taking a bath when I heard the doorbell. _____

2. while/we/play tennis/it/start raining

   _____

3. I/see an accident/while/I/wait for the bus

   _____

4. she/walk to school/when/she/meet her friend

   _____

5. our boss/talk on the phone/when/we/go into his office

   _____

6. my brother/come home/while/I/watch a movie

   _____

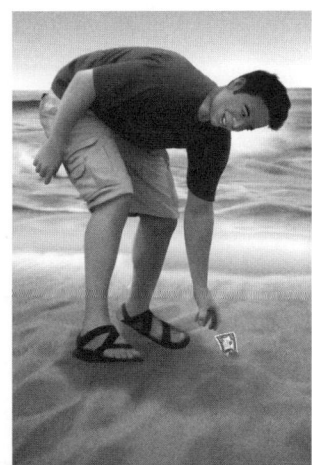

▲ Javier

C. Write sentences about these people using the simple past tense and past continuous tense.

1. _____

   _____

2. _____

   _____

▲ Mimi

Lesson B

A. Think about your biggest achievement, and fill in Column 1. Then think about a friend or family member with an important achievement, and fill in Column 2.

	Column 1: You	Column 2: Name:
1. What was the achievement?		
2. What were the steps in achieving this goal?		
3. What was the most difficult part of the achievement?		

B. Look at the achievements in exercise **A** and answer the questions.

1. Which achievement was more important? Why? _____

   _____

2. How do you feel about your achievement now? _____

   _____

3. Did your achievement change your life? Explain your answer. _____

   _____

C. Say each word out loud. Then check the column of the sound you hear.

	/t/	/d/	/Id/
1. learned			
2. talked			
3. discussed			
4. helped			
5. wanted			
6. used			
7. decided			
8. stopped			

Lesson C

A. Complete the sentences with a phrasal verb from the box. Be sure to use the correct tense.

| set out   give up   watch out   grow up   run out of   put up with   keep on |

1. We sometimes _____ coffee at home because we drink a lot of it and we forget to buy more.
2. I _____ in the country, and we always played outdoors all day when I was a child.
3. If you ride a bicycle in the street, you always have to _____ for cars.
4. Eric doesn't play the drums very well, but he _____ practicing because he really wants to play in a band some day.
5. It's only 100 meters to the top of this mountain. You can do it! Don't _____ now!
6. My apartment is very cheap, so I _____ all the noise from the busy street outside.
7. Subaru Takahashi _____ from Japan to cross the Pacific Ocean.

B. Write sentences with *too*, *enough*, or *not enough*.

1. Ali can't get a driver's license this year. (he/old) **He isn't old enough.** _____
2. I decided not to get a new computer. (it/expensive) _____
3. I can't hear the sound on the TV. (it/loud) _____
4. We're going to the beach to go swimming today. (the water/warm) _____
   _____
5. My little sister can cook spaghetti for dinner. (the recipe/easy) _____
   _____
6. I need something bigger to carry my books. (this backpack/big) _____
   _____
7. Diana isn't going to eat lunch today. (she/busy) _____
8. I never walk to school. (it/far from my house) _____

C. Oliver wants to walk across the Sahara Desert. Do you think he can do it? Write sentences with *too*, *enough*, or *not enough*.

1. (old) He's _____ to walk across the desert.
2. (strong) _____
3. (heavy) _____
4. (rich) _____
5. (your own idea) _____

▲ Oliver

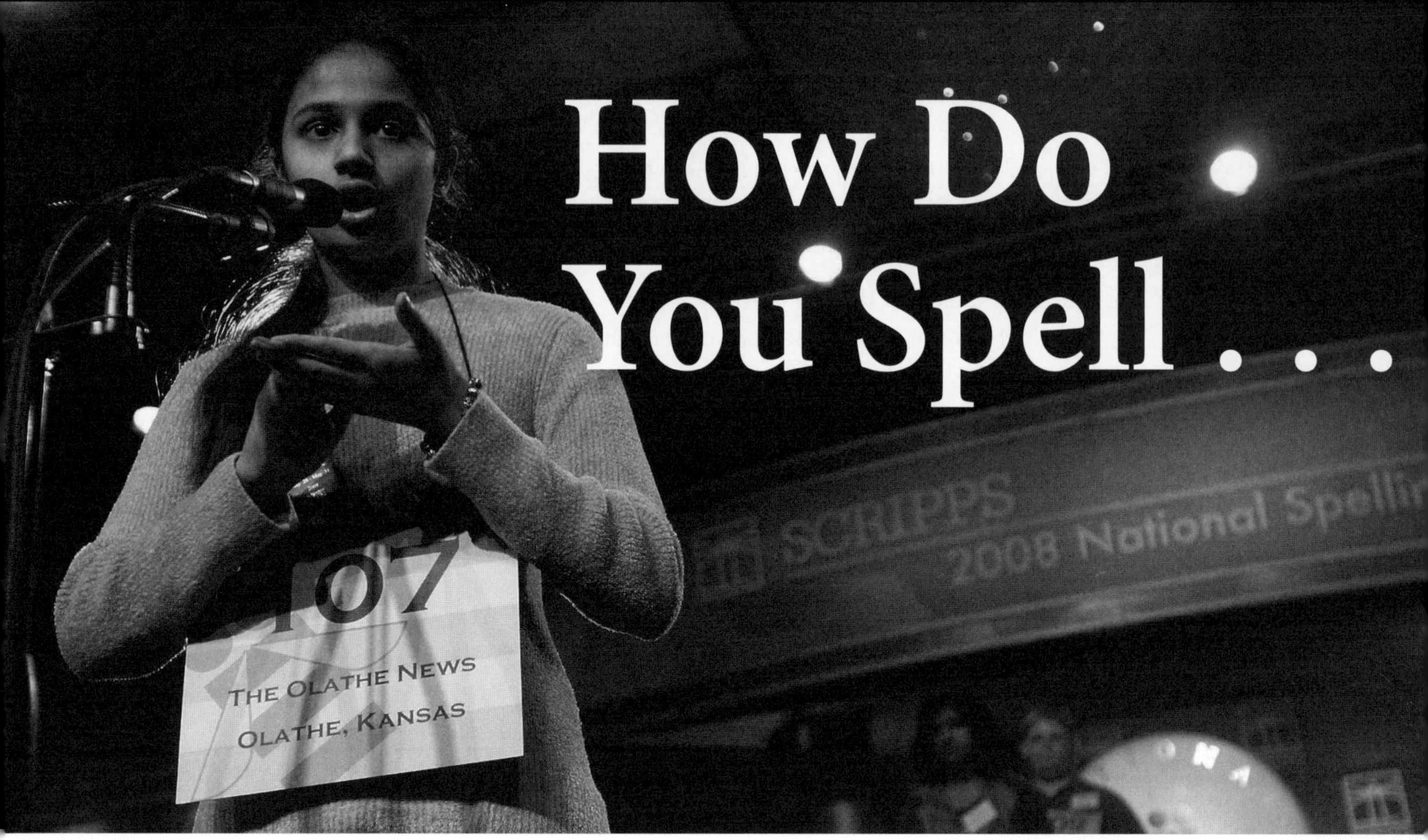

How Do You Spell . . .

Spelling English words isn't easy, but a boy in Indiana, USA, set a very difficult goal for himself. Thirteen-year-old Sameer Mishra wanted to become the best speller in the whole country and win the National Spelling Bee.

A spelling bee is a spelling contest for elementary school students in the United States. In a spelling bee, students stand in a line and spell words that the teacher pronounces. If they make a mistake, they must sit down. The last student who is standing is the winner. Every year, there are big spelling bees for cities and states. The winners go to the National Spelling Bee in Washington D.C.

This year, 288 students from the United States, Canada, and other English-speaking countries entered the National Spelling Bee. In the contest, students have to spell very long, difficult, and unusual words from a very large dictionary. Students spend months, or years, preparing. Sameer spent at least four hours every day learning new words. He studied 23 pages of the dictionary each day, and his sister helped him practice.

The final night of the National Spelling Bee was on TV. The students spelled 24 of the first 25 words correctly, including words like *brankursine*, *cryptarithm*, and *empyrean*. Then they started making mistakes. Finally, there were only two students in the contest: Sameer and a boy named Sidharth Chand. Sidharth made a mistake in the word *prosopopoeia*. To win, Sameer had to spell one more word correctly: *guerdon*. Sameer correctly spelled out "g-u-e-r-d-o-n" and became the best speller in America. (What does *guerdon* mean? A reward!)

Sameer won $40,000 to pay for his university education—he hopes to become a doctor. He has many other interests besides spelling. He plays the violin and enjoys video games. His parents are from India, and they are very proud of him. "I told my mom I was going to do the bee," Sameer said. "And if I was going to do it, I was going to win it one day."

A. Fill in the missing words to make a summary of the article.

A spelling bee is a contest for _____ students who speak English. They have to _____ difficult words. All the students stand up. The teacher says a _____. The first student has to _____ it. If the student spells the word wrong, he or she _____. At the end of the spelling bee, the winner is the _____ student who is standing. There are spelling bees for schools, _____, and states. Every year, there is a big national spelling bee in the city of _____. This year, the _____ was Sameer Mishra. He studied the dictionary for _____ hours every day!

B. Read the article again. Circle **T** for *true* or **F** for *false*.

1.	Sameer didn't make any mistakes in the spelling bee.	T	F
2.	The words in a spelling bee are words that we use every day.	T	F
3.	You can see a spelling bee on television.	T	F
4.	Students prepare for a long time before the National Spelling Bee.	T	F
5.	Sameer's family helped him before the spelling bee.	T	F
6.	Sameer won a violin and computer games in the National Spelling Bee.	T	F

C. Answer the questions.

1. How do you remember the spellings of English words? _____
   _____

2. How many new words can you learn in one day? _____

3. Do you think you could win a spelling bee? Why, or why not? _____
   _____

D. Write about a person you admire. What challenges did this person face? What did he or she achieve? Why do you admire this person?

_____

_____

_____

_____

_____

_____

_____

_____

▲ **Jenny Daltry and an Antiguan racer**

Review

Solve the crossword puzzle with vocabulary and grammar from this unit.

Across

1. I live in New York now, but I _____ in Hong Kong. (2 words)
4. You should _____ for dangerous animals in the jungle. (2 words)
7. I want to ___ White Mountain.
8. I'm 16, so I'm not old ___ to drive.
11. something that is new and difficult to do
15. I can't drink that coffee. It's ___ hot.
16. You need a lot of ___ to sail a small boat.
18. I always _____ money at the end of each month. (3 words)

Down

2. Jenny Daltry _____ insects and hot weather in her work. (3 words)
3. Running in a marathon is a ___ challenge.
5. succeed in doing something difficult
6. I _____ learning more English words every day. I never stop. (2 words)
9. something that you hope to do
10. Preparing for a big exam is a ___ challenge.
11. Subaru Takahashi ___ the Pacific Ocean.
12. surprising and wonderful
13. You need a lot of ___ to travel to the North Pole.
14. Learning to ski is difficult, but I won't _____. (2 words)
17. Two men _____ to walk to the North Pole in winter. (2 words)

Lesson A

A. Match the stage of life to the description.

1. infancy ____
2. old age ____
3. adulthood ____
4. adolescence ____
5. childhood ____

a. an adult
b. a baby
c. a teenager
d. a child
e. a senior citizen

B. When do most people do these things? Write the stage of life.

1. learn to talk __infancy_____

2. get married _____

3. stop working _____

4. have their first baby _____

5. learn to read _____

6. finish their education _____

C. Circle the correct form of each verb—simple past tense or present perfect tense.

1. I don't want to eat at Pizza Palace tonight. I (ate/have eaten) there twice this week.

2. Jessica (knew/has known) her best friend since they (were/have been) six years old.

3. I (worked/have worked) for this company since 1998, and I like it very much.

4. Marina (had/has had) a baby last month.

5. I (finished/have finished) my homework, so I can go out tonight.

6. We (saw/have seen) that video before. It (was/has been) terrible!

D. Have you done these things? If so, when did you do them for the first time? Write sentences with the present perfect tense and simple past tense.

1. __I've ridden a horse. I rode one in 2005. OR I've never ridden a horse.__

2. _____

3. _____

4. _____

5. _____

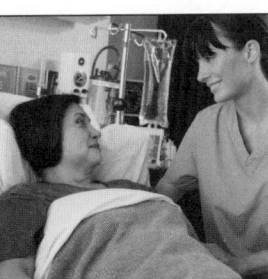

Lesson B

A. Unscramble the sentences to make a conversation.

(hear/you/the big news/did) (to drive/is/Mark/learning)

Beth: _____? _____.

(but/16/he's) (to/that's/too/young/drive)

Julia: _____! _____.

(about/oh/I/know/that/don't) (careful/very/he's) (teaching/and/his father/is/him)

Beth: _____. _____. _____.

(a few years/think/true/that's/but/I/he/wait/should)

Julia: _____, _____.

(the best age/well/to drive/what/do you think/is/to learn)

Beth: _____, _____?

(graduated high school/I think/people/should/their driver's license/after/get/they've)

Julia: _____.

B. Melissa is 15. She just got a job. Write a new conversation like the one in exercise **A**.

Your friend: _____

You: _____

Your friend: _____

You: _____

Your friend: _____

You: _____

C. Say these words out loud. Circle the unstressed syllables with the ə sound.

1. important
2. travel
3. pizza
4. apartment
5. animal
6. woman
7. listen
8. transition

Lesson C

A. Read the meanings and unscramble the expressions.

1. stopped working: (dertrie) _____
2. with the energy of a younger person: (flotuuyh) _____
3. between 30 and 39: (nirhetthrsiise) _____
4. acting like a child: (ilshidhc) _____
5. old enough to make good decisions: (tremau) _____
6. looking and acting old: (yeellrd) _____
7. between 40 and 60: (eilmdd-dega) _____

B. Read the sentences. Use *how* to ask questions about the underlined words.

1. My friend Lana is very <u>tall</u>.
   How tall is she? _____

2. My brother plays football really <u>badly</u>.
   _____

3. I just found out that Mr. Sloan is very <u>wealthy</u>.
   _____

4. I love to eat at Janie's house because she cooks so <u>well</u>.
   _____

5. The test was really <u>difficult</u>, and now I'm worried.
   _____

C. Ken has a new room mate, and his father is asking a lot of questions about him. Fill in his questions with *how*.

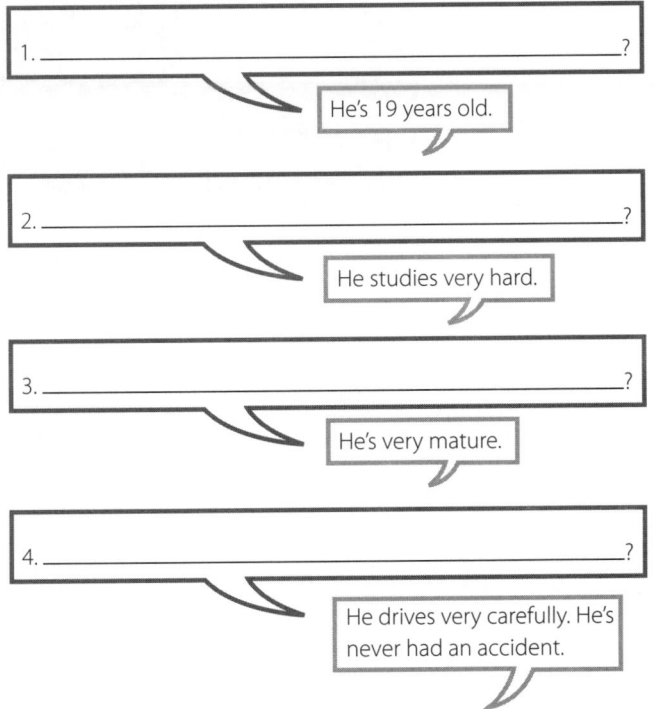

1. _____?

He's 19 years old.

2. _____?

He studies very hard.

3. _____?

He's very mature.

4. _____?

He drives very carefully. He's never had an accident.

5. _____?

He speaks English very well. He's spoken it all his life!

Celebrating Transitions

Every country has special celebrations to mark transitions in life. Here are three examples of important days for young people in different countries.

Do you remember your first day in school? Many children feel scared, but in Germany, the kids are very excited. Their first day in school, when they are six, is a big celebration called *Schulanfang*. All of the kids have new clothes, and their parents give them a *Zuckertuete*, a big colorful cone full of candy and small presents. Parents take pictures of their child holding the Zuckertuete. Then they meet their new teachers and classmates, and they sing songs and play games to celebrate. There is also a party for the parents after school with coffee and cake.

Girls in Mexico and other countries in Latin America are very excited when they turn fifteen. For them, it marks the transition from girl to young woman, and there is a special celebration called the *Quince Años*. The girl gets a beautiful and very expensive dress that looks a little bit like a wedding dress. In the evening, there is a huge party in a restaurant, with a big cake in the same colors as the girl's dress. People enjoy themselves until very late at night.

For young people in Japan, their twentieth birthday is very important, because that is when they become adults. There is a national holiday called Coming-of-Age Day to celebrate this. On the second Sunday in January, each city has a ceremony for people who had their twentieth birthday in the last year. All the new adults go to the City Hall to listen to speeches and get a present from the town's mayor. Everyone wears new clothes, and many women wear beautiful kimonos. Their families take lots of pictures.

A. Complete the chart with information from the reading.

Transition	*Schulanfang*	*Quince Años*	Coming-of-Age Day
Country			
Age of people celebrating			
When			
Where			
What do people do?			

B. Answer the questions.

1. Which of these celebrations sounds like the most fun? Why? _____
   _____

2. Which days are the most important in your country? Why? _____
   _____
   _____

C. Write about a celebration of a life transition such as a graduation or a wedding. Who was the party for? What was the person celebrating? Why was it important? What did you do at the party?

_____

_____

_____

_____

_____

_____

_____

Review

Solve the crossword puzzle with vocabulary and grammar from this unit.

Across

1. being a baby
5. Old enough to make good decisions
6. I (see) ___ that movie three times. I love it! (2 words)
7. finish your education
8. stopped working
10. elderly person (2 words)
13. 13–19 years old
14. I (do) ___ all my homework, so I can go out tonight. (2 words)
15. looking and acting old
16. having the energy of a young person

Down

2. being an adult
3. become husband and wife (2 words)
4. He's 20–29 years old. (3 words)
5. 40–60 years old
9. My brother ___ married last year.
11. acting like a child
12. get a different house or apartment
14. My sister ___ a child two years ago.

Lesson A

A. Complete the sentences with words from the box.

jewelry	silk	precious metals	precious stones
import	fur coat	export	pearls

1. Elena likes to wear a lot of _____. She always wears a necklace, bracelets, and several rings.
2. My country doesn't have any oil, so we _____ it from other countries.
3. That dress is really beautiful. It's made of _____.
4. Some people think it's bad to wear a _____ that's made from real animals.
5. Factories in my city make cars and _____ them to many countries.
6. Silver and gold are two _____.
7. The queen wore a necklace made of diamonds and other kinds of _____.
8. _____ come from oysters in Japan.

B. Rewrite these sentences in the passive voice.

1. One billion people speak Chinese. *Chinese is spoken by one billion people.*
2. The teacher checks all of our papers.

   _____
3. Japanese companies make a lot of cars.

   _____
4. French farmers grow the best grapes.

   _____
5. Teenagers write some computer programs.

   _____

C. Where do these things come from? Look at the map and write sentences in the passive voice.

1. gold/mine *Gold is mined in South Africa.* _____
2. coffee/grow _____
3. diamonds/find _____
4. pottery/make _____
5. movies/film _____
6. cotton/produce _____

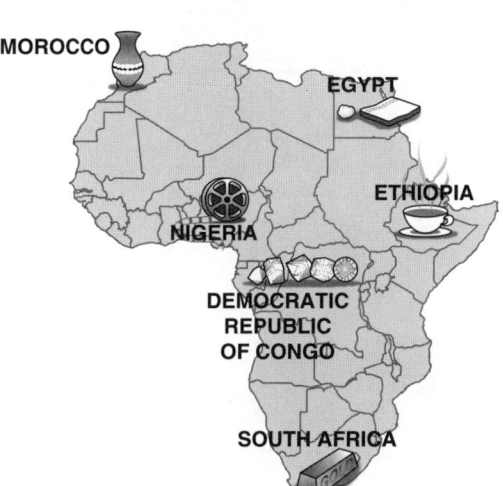

MOROCCO

EGYPT

ETHIOPIA

NIGERIA

DEMOCRATIC REPUBLIC OF CONGO

SOUTH AFRICA

Lesson B

A. What are three things you **need** in your life? Why do you need them?

1. _____ Reason: _____

   _____

2. _____ Reason: _____

   _____

3. _____ Reason: _____

   _____

B. What are things you **want** in your life? Why do you want them?

1. _____ Reason: _____

   _____

2. _____ Reason: _____

   _____

3. _____ Reason: _____

   _____

C. Match each word type with the examples. The content words are in **bold**.

1. **noun** __   a. write, ask
2. **main verb** __   b. the, an
3. **question word** __   c. can, will
4. **adjective** __   d. or, but
5. **adverb** __   e. been, were
6. pronoun __   f. I, them
7. auxiliary verb __   g. old, green
8. be __   h. happily, carefully
9. article __   i. after, under
10. prepositions __   j. when, why
11. conjunctions __   k. pizza, John

D. Underline the content words in the sentences. Then say the sentences out loud.

1. On Sundays, I can eat dinner with my family in the afternoon.
2. Those fur coats are expensive, but I don't think they're beautiful.
3. Alima is going to visit her cousins in Syria during her vacation.
4. Where did you put those new DVDs about animals?
5. We need bread, milk, and eggs from the store.
6. Andy is sad because he failed his big math test.

Lesson C

A. Write the past participle of these verbs. Be careful! Many of them are irregular. Use your dictionary if you're not sure.

1. make	*made*	9. steal	
2. take		10. grow	
3. use		11. mean	
4. write		12. check	
5. ask		13. spread	
6. spin		14. see	
7. fly		15. dig	
8. cook		16. fix	

B. Read the sentences and add a *by* phrase if the sentence needs it. Use your own ideas. Write OK if the sentence doesn't need a *by* phrase.

1. *Hamlet* was written **by William Shakespeare** _____
2. Coffee is grown in Mexico **OK** _____
3. The cake was baked _____
4. Toyota cars are made in Japan _____
5. My favorite movie was made _____
6. The homework was assigned for Monday _____
7. Last week, my bicycle was stolen _____
8. My brother was bitten _____
9. My house was built in 1890 _____
10. The telephone was invented _____

C. In your opinion, which of these things improves people's lives most? Number each thing from 1 to 4 with number 1 being the thing that improves people's lives most. Then explain your answers in one or two sentences.

1. _____ improves people's lives the most because _____
   _____

2. _____ improves people's lives the least because _____
   _____
   _____

money __

a nice house __

good health __

a good job __

Where Does Silk Come From?

It's hard to believe—but a beautiful silk dress comes from thousands of tiny worms! Silk, one of the world's greatest luxuries, is made by insects called silkworms. It takes about 5500 silkworms to make 2.2 pounds (1 kilogram) of silk. The process was discovered by the Chinese about 5000 years ago.

How is silk made? The process starts with the eggs of a certain kind of insect. The eggs are collected and kept warm. After a few days, the silkworms come out of the eggs. They are fed leaves from mulberry trees every 30 minutes, all night and all day. The sound of thousands of silkworms eating sounds like rain falling! The room is kept warm, and the silkworms must not be disturbed by loud noises or bad smells. After a month, they start to make a cocoon that looks like a fluffy white ball. After four days, the cocoon is ready.

The cocoons are heated, and the silkworms are killed inside them. Then the cocoons are put into water to make the silk loose. The silk from three or four cocoons is put together and made into a thread. One cocoon can make a thread 0.6 miles (1 kilometer) long! Finally, the silk threads are woven to make cloth, and the cloth is used for things like dresses, scarves, and neckties. Today, silk is produced in many countries, including India and Thailand, but more than 80 percent of the world's silk comes from China. Every year, enough silk thread is produced to go from the earth to the sun 300 times. People love silk clothes because they are beautiful and comfortable—silk feels cool in warm weather and warm in cool weather.

Now you know why silk is so expensive!

A. Number the pictures 1–8 to show the steps of making silk.

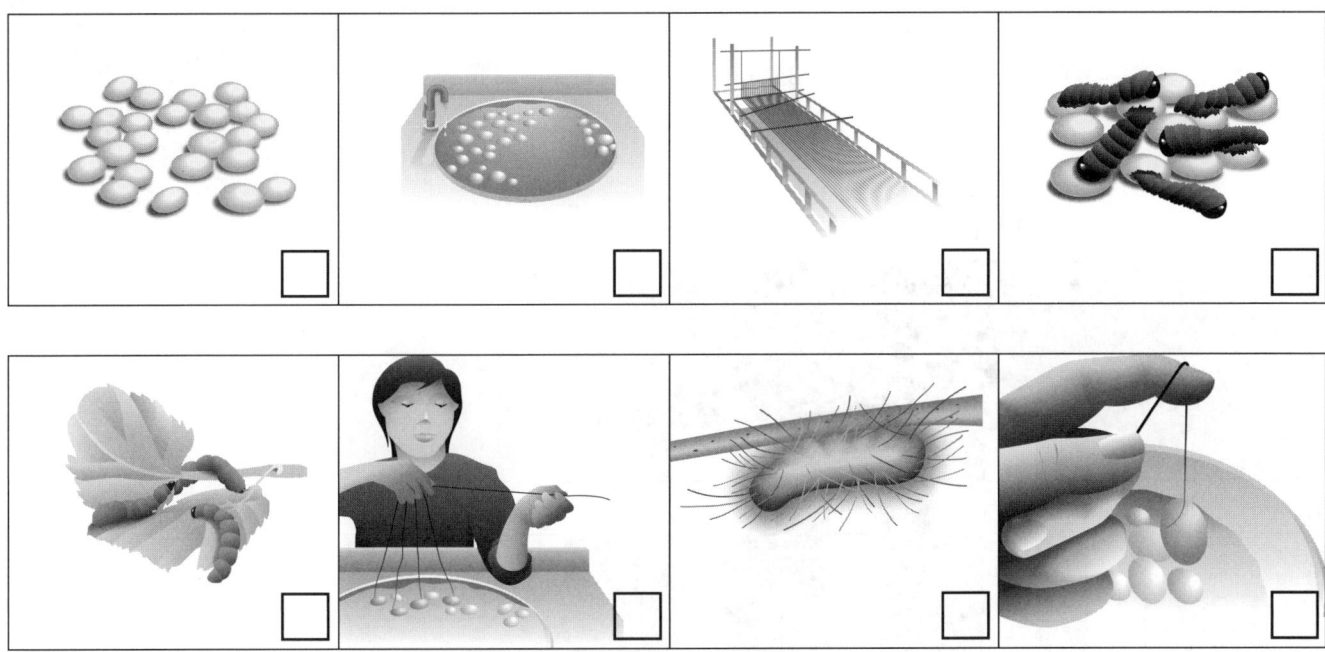

B. Answer the questions.

1. Why do people like to wear silk? _____
   _____

2. Do you use or wear anything made of silk? Why, or why not? _____
   _____

C. Imagine you have won a contest and you can choose your prize. Which of these luxuries do you want for your prize? Why?

a gold watch	1 kilogram of caviar	a diamond ring
1000 red roses	a painting by a famous artist	1 liter of perfume

_____

_____

_____

_____

_____

_____

Review

Solve the crossword puzzle with vocabulary and grammar from this unit.

Across

1. past participle of *fly*
6. rings, necklaces, and bracelets
8. buy from other countries
10. diamonds and rubies (2 words)
13. beautiful and expensive cloth
14. people use this to smell good
15. past participle of *mean*
16. past participle of *dig*
17. beautiful round white objects

Down

2. something expensive that you want
3. something that you need for life
4. gold and silver (2 words)
5. to make something better
7. sell in other countries
9. something to wear made from animal skin (2 words)
11. past participle of *steal*
12. past participle of *spread*
13. past participle of *spin*

Lesson A

A. Complete the sentences with words from the box.

species	habitat	predator	prey	hunt
wild	tame	protect	extinct	wildlife

1. You can't see dinosaurs at the zoo because they are _____.
2. The _____ of monkeys is jungles in warm countries.
3. Many tourists go to Africa to see _____ such as elephants, lions, and zebras.
4. A _____ is an animal that kills and eats other animals.
5. Sharks don't usually eat people. Their usual _____ is smaller fish.
6. In some countries, _____ dogs are a problem. They live in the forest and attack people!
7. In the past, rich people used to _____ tigers and use their skins for fur. Now there are very few tigers left.
8. You can see _____ elephants in the circus. They are friendly and live with people.
9. Save the Earth is an organization that tries to _____ animals and make national parks.
10. There are two different _____ of crocodiles in my country.

B. Fill in the correct form of each verb to talk about real conditions in the future.

1. If I _____ (have) free time this weekend, I _____ (call) you.
2. I _____ (go, not) swimming if you _____ (tell) me stories about sharks!
3. If Nita _____ (eat, not) more, she _____ (get) sick.
4. If we _____ (cut) down all the forests, the animals _____ (have, not) a place to live.
5. If I _____ (have) to cook dinner tonight, I _____ (make) spaghetti.
6. Tigers _____ (become) extinct if people _____ (stop, not) hunting them.

C. What will you do? Write sentences about these real conditions in the future.

1. **If I** _____

2. _____

3. _____

4. _____

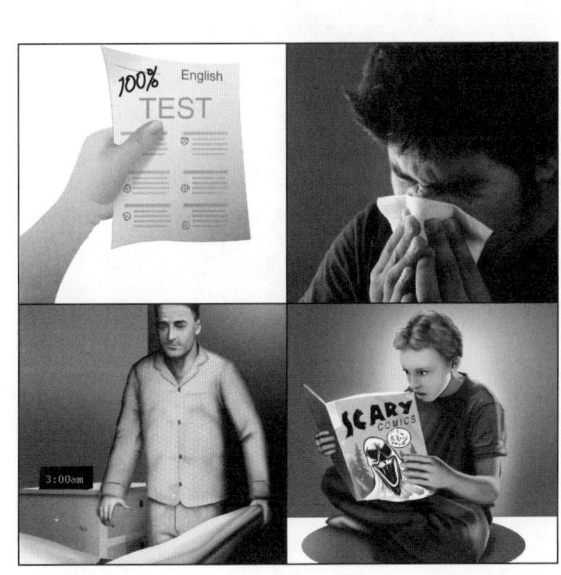

Lesson B

The city of White Beach is a very popular place for vacations. People go swimming there and stay in hotels near the beach. Yesterday, a lifeguard saw a big shark in the water. The shark stayed for a few minutes and then swam away. What should the city do? Today, authorities are talking about three different plans.

close the beach

put up a warning

![hunt the shark]

hunt the shark

A. Look at the plans. What will happen if the city does these things? Write sentences about possible situations.

Plan 1

    a. (hotels/lose money) If they close the beach, hotels _____

    b. (people/be unhappy) _____

    c. (your own idea) _____

Plan 2

    a. (people/not read it) _____

    b. (everyone/feel afraid) _____

    c. (your own idea) _____

Plan 3

    a. (it/be dangerous) _____

    b. (tourists/go home) _____

    c. (your own idea) _____

B. What should the city do? Choose plan 1, 2, or 3, *or* make your own idea. Explain your reasons.

_____

_____

_____

_____

C. Divide the sentences into phrases. Then read them out loud.

1. Amina and I went to the mall last weekend.
2. Do you have any brothers or sisters?
3. That new restaurant serves very bad food and terrible drinks.
4. I'll send you an email if I have time.
5. The zoo has three African elephants, four tigers, and two kangaroos.
6. I wash my face and brush my teeth when I get up.

Lesson C

A. Write the adverb for each adjective.

1. bad _____
2. angry _____
3. wonderful _____
4. slow _____
5. good _____

6. fast _____
7. loud _____
8. interesting _____
9. sad _____
10. lazy _____

B. How do you do it? Write sentences about yourself using adverbs.

1. walk **I usually walk quickly.** _____
2. read _____
3. swim _____
4. cook _____
5. run _____
6. speak English _____

C. Read the paragraph. Circle the correct quantifier.

I always carry 1. (too much/too many) things in my backpack. Of course, I have 2. (a lot of/much) books, because I'm a student! I have a really big dictionary with 3. (some/many) pages, so it's very heavy. And I carry 4. (too few/too many) notebooks—I have a different notebook for each class. I also like to bring 5. (a little/some) magazines to read between classes. Of course, I have 6. (a few/a little) cookies for a snack, and if I get thirsty, I have 7. (a few/a little) water in a bottle. And today I have 8. (a little/a lot of) CDs in my backpack—my friend wants to listen to them. My backpack probably weighs 10 kilos!

D. What's in your refrigerator right now? Make a list of things. Use quantifiers like *a few, some, a little, a lot of, many.*

1. _____
2. _____
3. _____
4. _____

5. _____
6. _____
7. _____
8. _____

Elephants or People?

"Last night, there were 20 elephants on my farm," says one man in Kenya. "We shouted and threw things to send them away, but they broke the fences and ate all my crops. What can I do?"

Elephants are fascinating animals, but they cause serious problems for the farmers near Mount Kenya National Park. The animals often leave the park and go into the farms outside it. There, they eat crops like corn and wheat and destroy houses. In one night, a family can lose all their crops—and their money for the year. Farmers have been hurt and even killed when they try to chase the elephants away.

"The problem began when more people came to Mount Kenya and started new farms," a government official explains. "The land was used by elephants in the past. At some times of the year, elephants go from one part of the area to another. They remember their old routes, and they walk through anything that's there—like a farm field or even a house. They also drink the water that is for the farm animals."

Farmers and their children used to sleep in their fields every night. If elephants came, they built fires or played drums loudly to scare them away. But the next day, the farmers were too tired to do their work. They spent most of their time and energy trying to keep elephants away from their fields. Then, a local organization found a better solution for this problem. They built electric fences to keep the elephants out. The electricity for the fences comes from the sun. The farmers have more time for their work, and children can go back to school. However, these fences are expensive to build, and the farmers must repair them often.

Now the government of Kenya has a new idea. It wants the people around the park to start businesses for tourists. People around the world love elephants, and many tourists want to see elephants close-up. The government hopes that this way, people and elephants will live together happily.

A. Write numbers next to the events in the order they took place.

___ The government made a plan to bring tourists to see the elephants.

___ People built electric fences to stop the elephants.

___ Elephants lived everywhere in Mount Kenya.

___ People came to Mount Kenya and started new farms.

___ People stayed in their farm fields to keep elephants away.

___ Elephants started walking through the farms and destroying them.

___ Farming became easier.

B. Match the sentence parts to show the reasons.

1. More people came to Mount Kenya ___
2. Elephants walk through the farms ___
3. The farmers shouted ___
4. The farmers were tired ___
5. Farmers have more time for work now ___
6. The government likes elephants ___

   a. because they bring visitors to Kenya.
   b. because the fences keep elephants out.
   c. because it was elephants' land in the past.
   d. because they were scaring elephants all night.
   e. because they wanted land for farms.
   f. because they wanted the elephants to leave.

C. In your opinion, what is the best solution for this elephant problem? Explain your answer.

_____

_____

D. Write about another kind of animal that causes problems for people. What do the animals do? How do people try to solve the problem?

_____

_____

_____

_____

_____

_____

Review

Solve the crossword puzzle with
grammar and vocabulary from this unit.

Across

1. able to continue for a long time
6. an animal that other animals eat
7. an animal that kills other animals for food
9. Kangaroos, koalas, and foxes are Australian ___.
10. There are too ___ books in my backpack.
11. adverb of *fast*
12. the place where an animal usually lives
15. keep safe
16. adverb of *good*

Down

2. a kind or type of animal
3. adverb of *bad*
4. Dinosaurs are ___. They are all dead now.
5. adverb of *easy*
8. I have a ___ of CDs in my bag.
12. try to find and kill animals
13. An animal that lives with people is ___.
14. If I have time, I ___ call you later.
16. An animal that lives in nature is ___.

Lesson A

A. Read the article and complete the text with words from the box.

sailing ships	Native Americans	cattle	New World	
Old World	Indians		colonists	tobacco leaf	explorers

Worlds in Contact

Before the 1500s, there was very little contact between people in the

(1) _____ countries like Spain and England and the areas

that became the (2) _____ countries like Mexico and the

United States. Then the first (3) _____ traveled across the

Atlantic Ocean in (4) _____. They thought they were in India,

so they called the people in the new lands (5) _____. Now

we call these people (6) _____. They learned about new

plants such as the (7) _____ and began to use them. Later,

people from Europe came to live in the new land. They were called

(8) _____. On their ships, they brought everything they needed

to live, such as (9) _____ and other farm animals.

B. Complete the sentences with *would* or *used to* and a verb from the box.

visit	play	have	travel	make	use

1. In high school, I _____ soccer every day after school.
2. The Maya Indians _____ a chocolate drink from cacao beans.
3. We _____ my grandparents every year on January 1.
4. A hundred years ago, people _____ by boat or on horses.
5. The Aztec people _____ salt to clean their teeth.
6. We _____ big dogs when I was a child.

C. Sara is talking to her grandfather about his childhood. Complete her questions with *used to* and a verb.

1. **Did you used to help** _____ your father with his work?
2. _____ a lot of rice every day?
3. _____ traditional clothes?
4. _____ to school?
5. _____ running water in your house?
6. _____ ? (your own idea)

Lesson B

A. This picture shows Inuit life in the past. Write sentences about these things with *used to*.

1. boats made of animal skins
   The Inuit used to use boats made of animal skins for hunting.

2. fur clothes
   _____

3. spear
   _____

4. sled
   _____

5. sled dogs
   _____

6. house made of snow
   _____

B. Think about daily life in your country 100 years ago. Write sentences about these things with *would*, *used to*, *didn't use to*, and the simple past tense.

1. food _____

2. clothes _____

3. schools _____

4. houses _____

5. medicine _____

6. entertainment _____

Lesson C

A. Write sentences by rearranging the phrasal verb.

1. The doctor says I should give up my favorite food.
   ___*The doctor says I should give my favorite food up.*___

2. I put my new shoes on before the party.
   _____

3. Jennie brought her little brother up after their parents died.
   _____

4. I help out my friends if they don't understand their classes.
   _____

5. When I wake up, I switch on my computer.
   _____

6. We wash our hands to keep away germs.
   _____

B. Who did it? Write past tense sentences in the passive voice.

▲ ancient Egyptians   ▲ Alexander Graham Bell ▲ William Shakespeare   ▲ Leonardo da Vinci   ▲ the Maya Indians

1. chocolate/make
   ___*Chocolate was made by the Maya Indians.*___

2. Macbeth/write
   _____

3. Great Pyramid/built
   _____

4. the telephone/patent
   _____

5. Mona Lisa/paint
   _____

C. What are some famous things that were made, written, invented, or discovered in your country? Who did them? Write past tense sentences in the passive voice. Use *by*.

1. _____
2. _____
3. _____

Living History at Jamestown Settlement

A woman in Native American clothes is sitting in the sun, sewing a dress from animal skin. Inside a building, a colonist is making a wooden chair, using very simple tools. And all around, tourists are taking pictures with their digital cameras. This is Jamestown Settlement today.

Jamestown, Virginia, was one of the first places in the world where people from Europe, America, and Africa came together, in 1608. Today, it's a living history museum, where children and adults come to experience history. In a living history museum, actors wear clothes from the past and demonstrate many of the activities of daily life back then. The actors also talk to the visitors and explain everything they do.

At a living history museum, there are always many things to touch, hear, and smell. Visitors at Jamestown Settlement can walk through copies of the three small sailing ships that carried colonists to Virginia and even lie down in a colonist's bed! The colonists stayed on the crowded, dangerous ships for more than four months. When they got to Virginia, they built an area of houses with a high wall around it. In today's fort, you can see houses, a church, and even a garden with foods that the colonists ate. Women in long dresses work inside their homes, and visitors can help them with their sewing and cooking.

There is also an Indian Village at Jamestown Settlement, and it looks very different from the fort. It shows how the Indians lived in long houses and grew corn and other crops in large fields. Actors there make pottery and teach visitors how to play Indian games. You can even help them make an Indian boat from a tree!

Today, the living history museum of Jamestown is very popular, especially with children and families. People come there to have fun, but also to learn. Many school classes visit to experience old ways of getting things done. A living history museum is the best way to understand how people lived in the past.

A. Read the article again. Circle **T** for *true* or **F** for *false*.

1. Tourists like to go to Jamestown today.   T   F
2. In Jamestown, people from three different cultures came together.   T   F
3. At a living history museum, all of the things to see are inside glass cases. T   F
4. Actors work at a living history museum.   T   F
5. The real ships that the colonists used are in Jamestown.   T   F
6. You can see a copy of an Indian village in Jamestown.   T   F
7. The Indians around Jamestown didn't know about farming.   T   F
8. The Jamestown Settlement now is only for learning.   T   F

B. Which of these things are found in the Jamestown Settlement now? Circle the things that are in the article.

people making pots	actors	archaeologists	ships
people cooking	dogs	people fighting with guns	Indian boats
an old school	staple foods	clothes that people used to wear	a fort

C. Answer the questions.

1. Are there any living history museums in your country? _____

   _____

2. Where are some places that foreign visitors can learn about your country's history?

   _____

   _____

D. Write about an important place in your country's history. What happened there? What can people see there today?

_____

_____

_____

_____

_____

_____

_____

_____

Review

Solve the crossword puzzle with vocabulary and grammar from this unit.

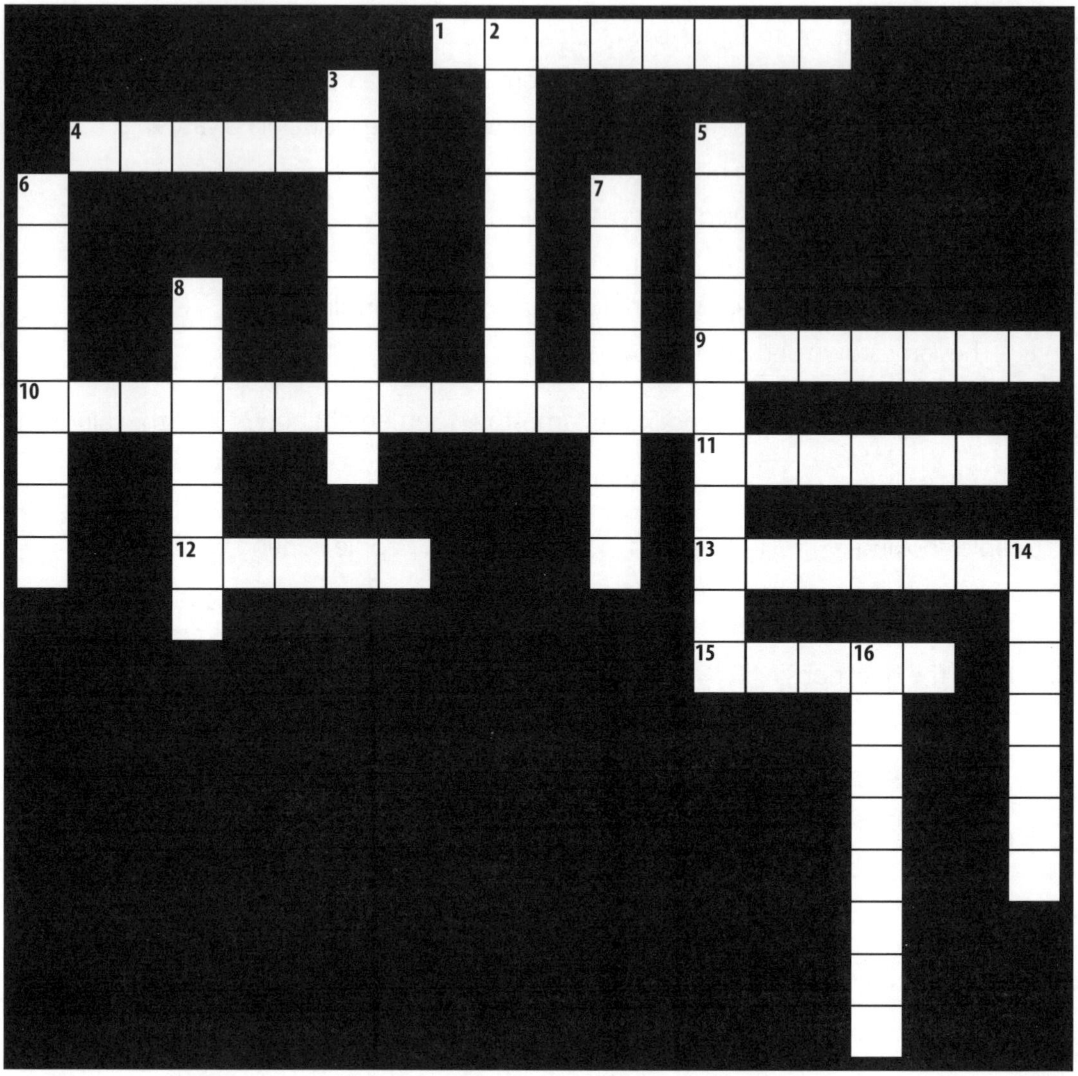

Across

1. America was the ___ ___ in the 1500s.
4. cows and bulls
9. Columbus thought he was in India, so he called the people ___.
10. another name for Indian
11. stop doing or having something
12. Did children ___ ___ go to school 100 years ago? (2 words)
13. do something good for someone
15. When you get dressed, you ___ ___ your clothes. (2 words)

Down

2. a person who travels to discover new places
3. make something stay far from you
5. In the 1600s, people came to America on a ___ ___. (2 words)
6. someone who has gone to live on new land
7. _____ the light. It's dark in here! (2 words)
8. raise a child
14. People smoke this in pipes.
16. Europe and Asia were the ___ ___ in the 1500s. (2 words)

Lesson A

A. Match the words with their meanings.

1. ecotourism __   a. looking at famous places
2. travel agent __   b. an injection that stops you from getting a disease
3. ticket __   c. a vacation trip to buy new things
4. visa __   d. a stamp or paper that allows you to enter a foreign country
5. beach vacation __   e. a worker who arranges trips for other people
6. itinerary __   f. a vacation trip to the seashore
7. passport __   g. a piece of paper that says you paid for a place on a train, airplane, etc.
8. shopping trip __   h. a vacation trip to enjoy and learn about nature
9. reservation __   i. a place that is saved for you in a hotel, airplane, train, etc.
10. vaccination __   j. a document that you must show when you enter or leave a country
11. sightseeing __   k. a plan for where you will go on a trip

B. Read the requirements for a tourist visa to the (fictional) country of Bertastan.
Write sentences about the requirements using the modals of necessity have to,
don't have to, or must.

REPUBLIC OF BERTASTAN
Tourist visa requirements:

1. form V-02 (filled out)

2. two photographs of your face (color, black-and-white)

3. photocopy of your plane ticket

4. pay $20 (cash or credit card)

5. Bring all documents to the Visa Office. Hours: 8 a.m. to 4 p.m., Monday to Friday

6. Normal time to receive your visa: two weeks

1. form **You have to fill out form V-02.** _____

2. color photographs _____

3. a photocopy of your plane ticket _____

4. cash _____

5. go to the Visa Office _____

6. go early in the morning _____

7. wait _____

C. What are some of the rules in your English class? Write sentences using *have to*, *don't have to*, or *must*.

1. **We must speak English every day.** _____

2. _____

3. _____

4. _____

Lesson B

A. Read the vacation brochure and complete the descriptions.

take a bus tour/hear lectures from famous professors/walk 10 miles
campgrounds in nature areas/student apartments/castles and old houses
college dining halls/local food/the finest restaurants

Spend this summer in Europe!

Adventure Vacation: Scotland!

Every day, you'll (1) _____ in the beautiful mountains. Every night, you'll stay in (2) _____. We'll eat (3) _____ and enjoy talking to local people. The perfect vacation for people who like plenty of exercise and fresh air!

Learning Vacation: Oxford University!

Would you like to try student life at the world's most famous university? In this summer program, you'll (4) _____ every day, and stay in (5) _____. In the evenings, we'll have dinner in (6) _____ where you can meet students from around the world.

Relaxing Vacation: Southern France!

We'll (7) _____ through the most beautiful towns, with plenty of time for shopping. At night, we'll stay in (8) _____ and famous houses. And every day, you'll have lunch and dinner in (9) _____.

B. Which of the vacations in exercise **A** would you enjoy the **most**? Explain your answer.

_____
_____
_____
_____

C. Which of the vacations in exercise **A** would you enjoy the **least**? Explain your answer.

_____
_____
_____
_____

Lesson C

A. Unscramble the words that match the meanings.

1. a card that shows your seat number on an airplane: drobagni saps _____

2. the part of an airport where travelers get their bags back: gggaabe imlac _____

3. a small bag that you can take on an airplane: racry-no agb _____

4. the part of an airport where travelers leave: speradtrue _____

5. a person who works for an airline at an airport: lairnei teang _____

6. the part of an airport where officers look for dangerous things: rucityse kechc _____

7. the part of an airport where travelers get on an airplane: tega _____

8. a large building in an airport: mertinla _____

9. the part of an airport where travelers come in: lariravs _____

10. where travelers show their tickets and give their bags to the airline: ckech-ni noucret _____

B. Complete the conversation with words from the box.

security check	carry-on bag	gate	flight	ticket	check	boarding pass

Check-in agent:	Good afternoon. Where are you flying to today?
Ahmed:	To Cairo. Here's my (1) _____.
Check-in agent:	Thank you . . . And do you have any bags to (2) _____?
Ahmed:	Yes, I have two. This is my (3) _____.
Check-in agent:	OK. Here's your (4) _____. You're in seat 14D. Boarding time is 3 p.m., but you must be at your (5) _____ 15 minutes before that.
Ahmed:	I have a question. Is there a gift shop after the (6) _____?
Check-in agent:	Yes, there is. Thank you, and enjoy your (7) _____!

C. Circle the correct modal in each sentence.

1. You (must/don't have to) get a passport before you go to another country.

2. Officers look in your bags because you (can't/have to) bring dangerous things on a plane.

3. You (must not/don't have to) bring food on that flight. Dinner is served on the plane.

4. At the airport, you (have to/don't have to) get a boarding pass before you get on your plane.

5. You (can't/don't have to) smoke tobacco on an airplane.

6. If you want to travel during a holiday, you (must/can't) make your reservations early.

D. What are some rules that visitors in your country should know? Write sentences with modals of necessity and prohibition.

1. _You have to take off your shoes when you go inside a house._

2. _____

3. _____

4. _____

Letters to the Editor

Today's topic: Should the city build a new Tourist Information Center?

1. The government must not spend money for useless things like a tourist information center. This city already has too many tourists. The streets are full of taxis and tour buses, and I have to stand up on the metro every day when I go to work. The beaches are always crowded. When I try to go shopping in my neighborhood supermarket, it's full of foreigners and I have to wait in long lines. A city is for its residents, not for tourists. If visitors want information, they can buy a guidebook! —*Carlo H.*

2. We should do more to help the tourists who come here. A lot of them are foreigners who don't speak our language, and they often have problems during their vacation. Tourists bring in a lot of money and give jobs to people in hotels, restaurants, and all kinds of shops. They also make our city a more interesting place. You can hear 10 different languages when you walk down the street and meet people from around the world. Tourists bring a lot of good things to our city. —*Mariam Y.*

3. We need to think about the kind of tourism we want to develop. We don't want people who will just go to the beach and then leave their garbage there when they go home. We're famous for our beaches, and that's why most people come here. But we also have wonderful museums and places for sightseeing. Too many visitors just go to the beach and don't learn anything about our country and our culture. We have to do more to help them enjoy their time here. —*Lee F.*

A. Read the letters to the editor. Write the numbers by the titles.

___ Be careful about tourism

___ Good for the city

___ Too many visitors!

B. Which of the writers would agree with these statements? One, two, or three answers may be correct.

	Carlo	Melissa	Lee
1. We should build a new tourist center.			
2. Tourists sometimes cause problems.			
3. Tourists do good things for our city.			
4. The city would be better with fewer tourists.			
5. Tourists should learn about the places they visit.			
6. We shouldn't do more to help tourists.			
7. Tourists have a big effect on this city.			
8. There are good and bad kinds of tourism.			

C. Circle one statement in **B** that you agree with. Why do you agree?

_____

_____

D. Should your country (or your city) try to get more tourists? Write about your answer and explain your reasons.

_____

_____

_____

_____

_____

_____

_____

Review

Solve the crossword puzzle with
vocabulary and grammar from this unit.

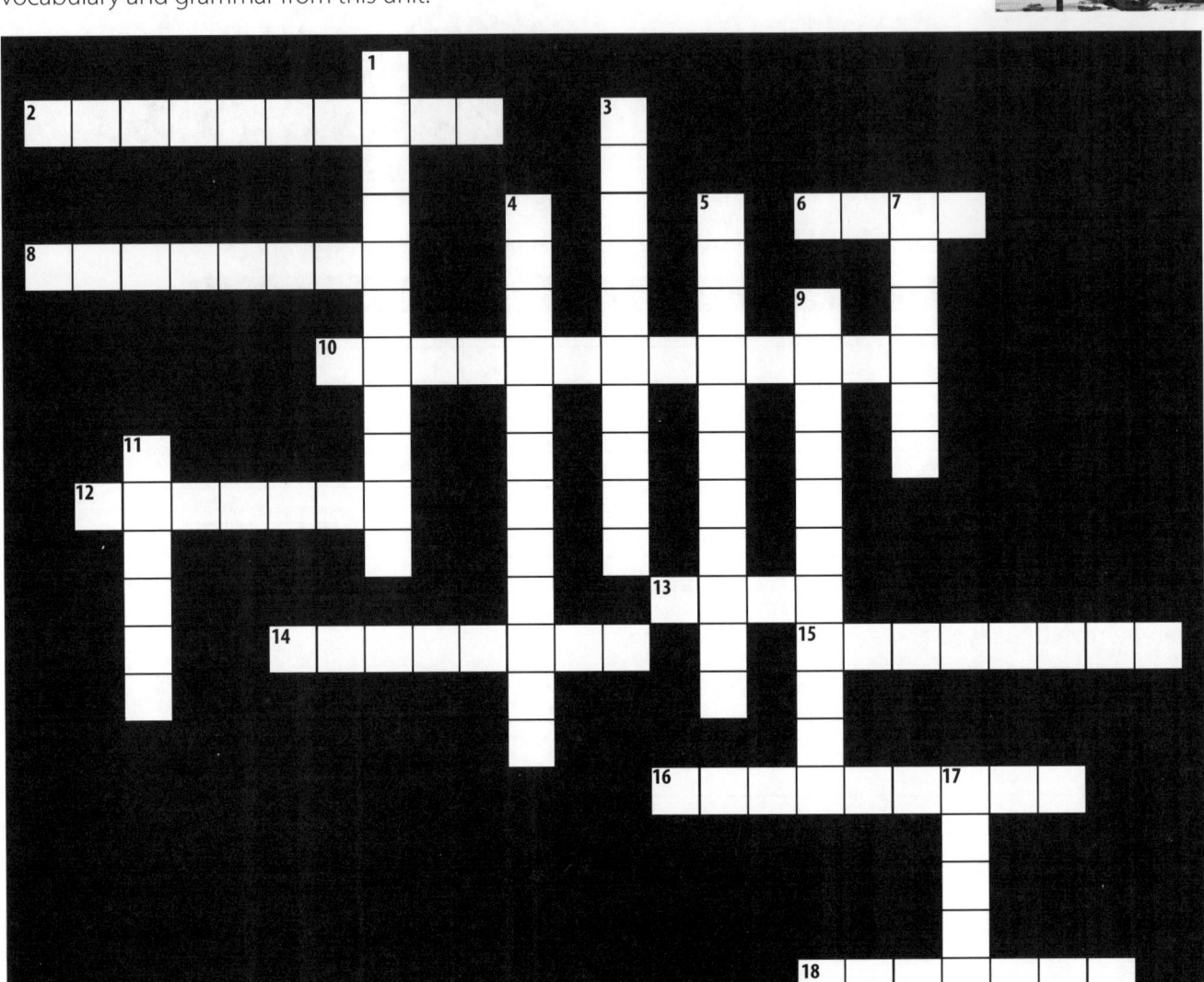

Across

2. travel in nature
6. where you get on the plane
8. a travel document with your name and photo
10. where officers look for dangerous things in bags
12. This is my ___-___ bag for the airplane.
13. a paper that says you can enter one country
14. where travelers come into the airport
15. an airport building
16. a plan for a trip
18. You ___ ___ take a gun on an airplane! (2 words)

Down

1. looking at famous places
3. where travelers go out from the airport
4. a card that shows your seat number on the air-plane
5. get this so you won't become ill
7. a paper that shows you've paid for a trip on a plane, bus, etc.
9. a place saved for you in a hotel, plane, etc.
11. You ___ ___ buy a ticket to get on an airplane. (2 words)
17. The airline ___ works at the airport.

Lesson A

A. Complete the sentences with words from the box.

employee	assistant	boss	qualifications
volunteer	training	experience	owner

1. I am the _____ to the sales manager. I help him do his work.

2. Angela is a _____ at her son's school. She helps the children with their classes, but she doesn't get any money for it.

3. Brad has good _____ for any job in an office. He has excellent computer skills, and he has worked for two large companies.

4. Ms. Baker has 10 years of _____ as a sales representative.

5. My brother is the _____ of an Italian restaurant.

6. This summer I am going to take a _____ program so I can get a job in a hospital.

7. I asked my _____ for a day off from work next Monday.

8. Shawn is a new _____ of the company. He started working here two weeks ago.

B. Circle the modal that best completes each sentence.

1. I think Andy (should/had better not) take a computer course. He could get a better job.

2. You (had better not/should) come to work late again. Our boss looked really angry this morning!

3. Mark (ought to/shouldn't) eat so much candy if he has problems with his teeth.

4. You (had better not/ought to) tell your father about your car accident before he sees the car.

5. You really (should/had better) try this chocolate cake. It's delicious!

C. Your friend is looking for her first job. Give her advice, using modals.

1. should I think you should get a nicer haircut. _____

2. shouldn't _____

3. ought to _____

4. had better _____

5. had better not _____

Lesson B

A. Mike is talking to a career advisor about jobs. Unscramble the questions about jobs and write them on the lines.

1. other people/with/do/you/to/work/like

   Advisor: _____ ?

   Mike: Yes, I do. I get bored if I work alone.

2. you/salary/is/your/important/to

   Advisor: _____ ?

   Mike: I need a good salary because I have to help my parents.

3. a/want/you/lot of/do/vacation time

   Advisor: _____ ?

   Mike: I don't need much vacation time if I enjoy my work.

4. need to/you/near/work/your home/do

   Advisor: _____ ?

   Mike: Not really. I have a car, so I can drive to work.

B. Choose the best job for Mike and explain your answer.

sales representative   artist   computer programmer   health care worker

_____

_____

_____

_____

C. Lingua School is looking for an English teacher for children. Write three questions that the school might ask job applicants.

1. _____
2. _____
3. _____

In *yes/no* questions, the speaker's voice rises on the last content word. In *wh-* word questions, we use a rising then falling intonation over the last content word.

D. Circle the last content word in each question. Then read the sentences out loud.

1. Is she in your class?
2. When is your interview?
3. Why did you call me?
4. What did the man ask about?

5. Have you seen that new movie?
6. Can you speak Japanese?
7. Did you go to the party with her?
8. Where did you leave your car?

Lesson C

A. Two kindergarten teachers are talking. Complete their conversation with *-ing* and *-ed* adjectives made from words in the box. Use each word once.

bore surprise satisfy terrify interest please

Adam: So, how was your first day?

Cassie: It was great! I felt so nervous at first, I was really (1) _____. But after that, I enjoyed it. The kids are great.

Adam: What did you do with them?

Cassie: First they drew pictures, and then they told stories about the pictures. The stories were so (2) _____that I wanted to write them down!

Adam: Did the head teacher come in to see your class?

Cassie: Yes, he did, and he was very (3) _____. He said I'm doing well. I was really (4) _____. I thought I would have a lot of problems, but it went very well.

Adam: Teaching young children is really (5) _____because they learn so fast.

Cassie: I'm sure I'll never be (6) _____.

B. Complete the sentences with indefinite pronouns (*no one, everybody, something, anyone,* etc.).

1. _____ knows what time the dinner is, because Peter forgot to tell us.

2. I'm sorry, I can't help you with your homework. I don't know _____ about science.

3. _____ called while you were at the library, but he didn't tell me his name.

4. I didn't have time to put away the groceries, so I left _____ on the kitchen table.

5. My eye really hurts. I think there's _____ in it.

6. _____ really enjoyed the show. They all said it was very, very funny.

7. The box was empty. There was _____ in it.

C. Complete the conversation with your own ideas.

Your friend: What will you use English for after you finish this class?

You: I'm planning to _____ .

Your friend: You sound happy about that.

You: I am! _____

_____

Your friend: That sounds great! I need to start thinking about my future too.

You: You really should _____

_____

Dream Jobs: Mona Davis

Mona Davis is sitting in a theater, eating a chocolate bar and laughing very loudly at the movie. After a few minutes, she takes out a notebook and writes down a few words. For her, it's just a normal day at work.

Mona is the movie critic for *Tonight Magazine*. Every week, she writes about all the new movies and gives them ratings from **** (excellent) to * (awful). She sees at least two movies every day, even though she doesn't write about everything she sees. "I only write reviews of the most important movies—good or bad!"

It's a dream job, but Mona needed special qualifications to get it. She studied filmmaking in college and made short movies for her classes. "I've always loved watching movies," she says. "And it's fun to see a new movie, before anyone has seen it."

Mona works hard. Some days, she sees three or even four movies in a row—starting in the afternoon and finishing at midnight. It's not always easy to stay awake for the last movie. "Sometimes I need a big cup of coffee during the evening," she says. She makes notes about each movie immediately after she sees it. Then, the next day, she writes her reviews in the afternoon—before going to see more movies!

The job does have a negative side, too. She often gets emails from people if they don't agree with her opinions. "Last week," she says, "a woman sent me a very angry 10-page letter because I said her favorite actor's new movie was awful."

But Mona really enjoys her job. She says, "I'm happy when I can get more attention for movies made by young actors and filmmakers. Sometimes I can really help their careers. And it's great that so many people read my reviews every week in *Tonight*. I'm not famous, but millions of people enjoy my work!"

A. Complete the chart about this dream job. Use your own words.

Name	
Job	
Qualifications	
Job duties	watch write
Good things about job	can see can help
Bad things about job	sometimes feels people

B. Is Mona's job a *dream job* for you? Explain your answer.

_____

_____

_____

C. Write about someone who has a great job. It can be someone you know or a famous person. Why is it a great job? What are this person's job duties? How did this person become qualified for the job?

_____

_____

_____

_____

_____

_____

_____

Review

Complete the crossword puzzle with vocabulary and grammar from this unit.

Across

2. the qualities and skills that you need to do a job
7. someone with a business that belongs to him or her
8. Do you know ____ about ethnobotany?
9. someone who works for no money because he or she wants to
10. knowledge that you have from doing something
13. feeling not interested
15. I called, but ____ answered the phone.
16. education to do something

Down

1. a person who works taking care of his or her house
3. someone who helps another person do work
4. feeling strong fear
5. something that meets your wants or needs
6. someone who works for a company or a person
11. the person in charge of others
12. There's ____ in the refrigerator. It's empty.
14. ____ in my class likes our teacher because she's so nice.

CELEBRATIONS

Lesson A

A. Complete the sentences with words from the box.

holiday	celebrate	exciting	festival	take place
colorful	crowd	participate	well-known	annual

1. I play the violin in the city orchestra, so I _____ in the city music fair every year.
2. Hogmanay parties _____ in Edinburgh and other cities in Scotland.
3. In some countries, people _____ the first day of summer with big fires in the evening.
4. At the Carnival parade, there were more than 50,000 people in the _____.
5. Carnival in Brazil is a very _____ celebration. It's famous all over the world.
6. Eid al Fitr is my favorite _____.
7. The Winter Fair is a/an _____ celebration in my city. It takes place every year in January.
8. Rosa wore a very _____ dress for the National Day parade. It was green, yellow, and red, the colors of our flag.
9. Next year we will have a film _____ at our university. We will have three days of movies and talks by famous actors.
10. The Spring parade is very _____ for children. They love to see the floats and they get lots of candy.

B. Write sentences comparing these two brothers with (not) as . . . as.

1. tall **Dale is not as tall as Mike** _____
2. old **Dale** _____
3. heavy _____
4. intelligent _____
5. busy _____
6. happy _____

Dale (14) and Mike (16)

C. Make an advertisement for a celebration in your city or country.

Come and celebrate _____ with us! It's well-known because _____
_____. You'll see colorful _____
_____. You can participate in _____
_____. The _____ is/are exciting. It's as _____
as _____.
It takes place _____. Don't miss it!

Lesson B

A. Complete the chart with information about two holidays in your country.

Holiday name	1.	2.
When does it take place?		
How do people celebrate?	* * *	* * *
Where do people celebrate?		
What are the special foods?		

B. Think about the holidays you wrote about in exercise **A**. Which one is more interesting for foreign visitors? Explain your answer.

_____

_____

_____

_____

In questions with choices, the intonation goes down on the last choice and up on all the other choices.

C. Mark the intonation in these questions with arrows ↗ ↘. Then say the sentences out loud.

1. Should we watch the video tonight or tomorrow?

2. Would you like fish, chicken, or pasta?

3. Do you want to make an appointment for Monday, Tuesday, or Wednesday?

4. Would you rather study in Canada or England?

5. What kind of pizza do you want—vegetable, chicken, pineapple, or cheese?

Lesson C

A. Unscramble the greetings for these days.

1. (sshwie steb) _____

2. (edi akbmuar) _____

3. (enw phayp arye) _____

4. (ypahp yaneanvris) _____

5. (insnarglatuocot) _____

B. Write questions about these days. Then write your answers.

1. New Year's Eve/go out/stay home

   On New Year's Eve, would you rather go out or stay home?

   I'd rather go out.

2. your anniversary/get emails/get anniversary cards

   _____

   _____

3. the last day of English class/take a test/have a party

   _____

   _____

4. your vacation/relax/do something exciting

   _____

   _____

5. the next holiday/spend time with your family/see all your friends

   _____

   _____

C. Think about a celebration you **don't** enjoy. What do people usually do? What would you rather do? Why?

_____

_____

_____

_____

> For the Autumn Holiday, people usually travel to their hometown. I would rather stay home, because the highways are very crowded and you can't get a train or bus ticket.

The Oldest Celebration in the World

The summer solstice is the longest day of the year. On that day (around June 21 in the northern half of the world) the sun is the highest in the sky, so the earth gets the most hours of light. People in many countries celebrate that day in a holiday called Midsummer.

Thousands of years ago, summer was the happiest time of the year in the northern countries. The snow was gone, the air was warm, the crops were planted, and food was easier to get. People celebrated Midsummer and did many different things. In many cultures, they built big fires and jumped over them. They thought that the fire would make the sun's energy stronger and help the crops grow faster. In some places, people believed that the crops would grow as high as people could jump. Women and girls would swim in rivers to bring rain for the crops.

Today, Midsummer is still celebrated in many countries. In towns in Sweden, people put up a Midsummer Pole made of wood covered with flowers. They dance around it and sing. Afterwards, they eat fish, new potatoes, and strawberries. That night, young people pick seven different flowers and put them under their pillow when they sleep to dream about the person they will marry.

In Finland, people go out to the country and build huge fires to celebrate Midsummer. People get together with their friends for a big celebration all night. Because Finland is so far north, the sky is light most of the night on Midsummer. Many Finnish people start their summer vacation on that day.

In some parts of Spain, people have fireworks on the beaches at night to celebrate Midsummer. Some people believe that plant medicines work the best if they are made on Midsummer, so women go out to collect the plants that night. Some people put the plants in water and then wash their faces with the water for good health. And of course there are special foods: fish, potatoes, and corn bread.

A. Read the article again. Circle **T** for *true* or **F** for *false*.

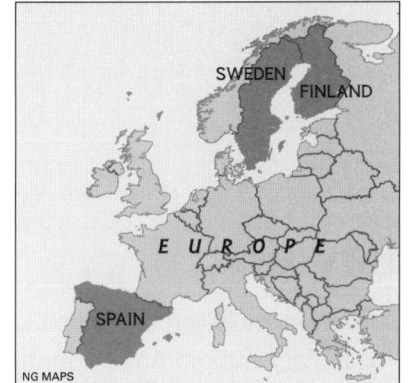

1. Midsummer celebrates the most difficult time of the year.   T   F
2. Midsummer is the shortest night of the year.   T   F
3. In the past, Midsummer was an important holiday for farmers.   T   F
4. Midsummer fires were a symbol of the sun.   T   F
5. Midsummer customs are the same in all countries.   T   F
6. Now, Midsummer is mostly a holiday for having fun.   T   F

B. Circle the places where people do these things for Midsummer. One, two, or three answers may be correct.

1. Eat special food   Sweden   Finland   Spain
2. Go to the beach   Sweden   Finland   Spain
3. Try to find out about the future   Sweden   Finland   Spain
4. Do special things for their health   Sweden   Finland   Spain
5. Celebrate at night   Sweden   Finland   Spain

C. Write about a special holiday in your country. How do people celebrate? What do you enjoy most?

_____

_____

_____

_____

_____

_____

_____

_____

_____

_____

Review

Solve the crossword puzzle with vocabulary and grammar from the unit.

Across

3. makes you feel happy and enthusiastic
5. clothes for a special day or occasion
6. bright, with many colors
9. famous
12. greeting for a graduation
13. every year
14. happen (2 words)
15. a time with many performances of music, dance, etc.
16. a day when people don't work

Down

1. a greeting for a wedding (2 words)
2. many people together
4. do something enjoyable for a special day
7. take part in
8. They've been married for ten years. Happy ____
10. I don't want to go out. I ____ stay home. (2 words)
11. greeting for January 1.

VOCABULARY INDEX

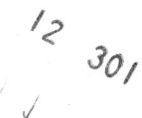

12 301